TRUMP

NEVER
GIVE UP

TRUMP
NEVER
GIVE UP

How I Turned
My Biggest
Challenges into
Success

DONALD J. TRUMP

with Meredith McIver

WILEY

John Wiley & Sons, Inc

Published by John Wiley & Sons, Inc., Hoboken, New Jersey.
Published simultaneously in Canada.

For general information on our other products and services or for technical support,
please contact our Customer Care Department within the United States at
(800) 762-2974, outside the United States at (317) 572-3993 or fax (317) 572-4002.

Wiley also publishes its books in a variety of electronic formats. Some content that
appears in print may not be available in electronic books. For more information
about Wiley products, visit our web site at www.wiley.com.

Library of Congress Cataloging-in-Publication Data:

Trump, Donald, 1946–
    Trump never gice up: how I turned my biggest challenges into success /
Donald Trump with Meredith McIver.
        p.   cm.
    ISBN 978-0-470-19084-5 (cloth)
    1. Success in business   2. Business failures   3. Management   4. Trump,
Donald, 1946– I. McIver, Meredith. II. Title.
    HF5386.T81484   2008
    658.4′092—dc22

                                                                2007033359

Printed in the United States of America.

SKY10078171_062424

To my parents,
Mary and Fred Trump

CONTENTS

CONTENTS

Contents

CONTENTS

Contents

CONTENTS

ACKNOWLEDGMENTS

It is a pleasure to work with my team at the Trump Organization, which includes my chief assistant, Rhona Graff, my co-author Meredith McIver, and our photo coordinator, Kacey Kennedy. Your efforts and efficiency make my job much easier, and I'm grateful for your help. I'd also like to mention other members of the Trump Organization who helped, namely Allen Weisselberg, Ivanka Trump, Andy Weiss, George Sorial, and Jeff McConney. Your dedicated work is greatly appreciated. A special thanks to Julius Schwarz of Bayrock and to Jim Fazio.

To the Trump University team: This collaboration has been as enjoyable as our first, *Trump 101: The Way to Success*, and I'd like to thank Michael Sexton and his very fine team for their outstanding performance.

To Richard Narramore, senior editor of John Wiley & Sons, and Miriam Palmer-Sherman, production manager, my thanks for your continued and excellent work. I also want to acknowledge Mike Freeland, cover designer.

DONALD J. TRUMP

INTRODUCTION

WHAT GOES THROUGH MY MIND WHEN I HEAR THE WORD "NO"

This book is about a subject near and dear to my heart—never giving up. Needless to say, I have a lot of experience in this area, so I feel I have some insight on the subject. I've written a number of books already, and I don't need the money, but it's a subject I feel strongly enough about to take the time to write about it.

The first big "No" that hit me came when I was first starting out in Manhattan in the 1970s, and everyone—and I mean *everyone*—told me that it was a terrible time for real estate. Even people who were well established were saying that. What they were saying was true—the market had definitely cooled, and there was no denying that fact. Even worse, there was serious talk about New York City going bankrupt. Then the federal government announced a moratorium on housing subsidies. The city had been receiving them in abundance, and suddenly, that was no more.

If I'd only considered the facts, which weren't too rosy, there is no way I would have ventured into real estate. But I did. Why? Because when I hear the word "No" it becomes a challenge to me. I believe the so-called impossible is actually very often possible, if you're willing to work very hard, and if you realize that problems can become opportunities. New York City was having problems, but maybe I could do something about those problems. That kind of attitude can give you the power to conquer obstacles and succeed in the face of long odds. I want this book to help you do just that.

As I went along, I realized that every project came with its own set of major challenges, and I began to learn to expect them. That was okay because I was prepared. That's another reason I'm writing *Never Give Up*—to let you know you should be prepared and to try to help you with the situations you might encounter. Our experiences will not be the same, but I've learned a great deal from reading about other people and history and by applying what I've learned to my own circumstances. My hope is that you will do the same. Learn from my problems and experiences, and you'll do a better job of anticipating and solving your own. And remember, the way I see it, the bigger the problem, the bigger your chance for greatness.

One thing I've learned is that discouragement should not be tolerated for very long. It's okay to get fed up a bit and maybe gripe for a minute or two. Personally, I like to go golfing when I'm stressed or just swing a club in my office. But feeling negative should be a very temporary state of mind. It's hard, but there is a form of mental courage that can be cultivated—and you will see in the following chapters some examples of how I dealt with some pretty big blows and setbacks. Of course, a lot of things are just irritating—so don't be surprised and don't overestimate them in your mind. Learn to put them in perspective. You'll see in this book how I learned to do that.

Having confidence in yourself is key to being resilient and staring adversity in the face. This book is dedicated to giving you that foundation of confidence—and the ability—and desire—to never give up!

See you in the winner's circle.

DONALD J. TRUMP

1

THE LOWEST MOMENT
IN MY LIFE AND HOW I
FOUGHT BACK

A Billion Dollars in the Hole

What do you do when the entire world tells you it's over? I had such an amazing reversal of fortune in the early 1990s that I am listed in the *Guinness Book of World Records* for the biggest financial turnaround in history. I don't recommend anyone aim for the same goal, but when you've been on the financial high wire, it gives you a certain perspective that might be helpful to other people.

It's been said that what makes me accessible to people—aside from *The Apprentice* showing how I operate in the business world—is that I've faced tremendous adversity. It's something just about everyone can relate to. The difference may be in the amount of zeros after the numbers, but the point is, people can relate to difficulties. I don't think anyone gets away with a challenge-free life experience. As one writer described the journey of life, "No one gets out of this alive." That's a bit existential but when you're down a few billion dollars in the red, it can make you think in new dimensions.

My situation in the early 1990s wasn't looking great. I had billions in loans I couldn't pay, and I had personally guaranteed $975 million of that debt. I could easily have gone bankrupt. This shouldn't surprise anyone because I'd always done things in a big way, and so it follows that my highs would be followed by a suitably low low. That was a tremendous low. The banks were after me. People avoided me. There was a recession, and the real estate market was almost nonexistent. This was not a good scenario.

Then in March of 1991, both the *Wall Street Journal* and the *New York Times* ran front page stories—on the same day!—detailing my predicament and the total financial ruin that would happen any moment. The radio stations got the story and the loss of my empire was big news around the world. They were sure I was finished. It would have made a fantastic story—except that it was happening to me.

That was the lowest moment I had yet encountered in my life. The phones in my office were even quiet, which had never happened before. In fact, I suddenly had a lot of quiet time to think, and I reviewed the situation objectively. It became clear to me that part of what got me into this situation was that I had lost my perspective and started to believe the news stories about me having "the Midas touch" when it came to business. In other words, I had become complacent. My momentum wasn't where it should have been.

However, *giving up* is something that never entered my mind. Not for one second, and that's one reason I think I confounded my critics. They were trying to skewer me, but it had the opposite effect—it just made me want to make a comeback and in a big way. I knew I could prove them wrong by being stubborn, being tenacious, and not giving in or giving up. I became a stronger person very quickly during this time. I'm not advising you to ask for the same pressure, but know that if you meet with some setbacks, refusing to give up is probably your best strategy.

What gave me this fortitude? I'm not sure, but being tossed aside as a "has-been" or a "wash-up" by the world press might have had something to do with it. I'd also already learned that problems are often opportunities in disguise. I began to see my situation, believe it or not, as a great opportunity. I had a big chance to show the press and my critics and enemies that I was a force to be reckoned with, not a flash-in-the pan success with no staying power. That's heady incentive, and that's looking at the situation positively.

Then there was a turning point, and that turning point was my attitude. My accountants still remember the night they were in the conference room until all hours in the woe-is-us mode, and I suddenly walked in to tell them about all the new projects I had lined up for us. There were a lot of projects, and they were big deals. I was in an exuberant mood, and my descriptions were colorful and optimistic. They thought I had cracked, that maybe I was beginning to hallucinate from the pressure, but I had reached a point where I knew it was time to move forward. It wasn't an act I put on—I was ready. All this financial pressure would be behind us in a short amount of time, I told them. I believed it, too.

As it turns out, that was indeed the turning point. All of us decided to focus on the solution and not the problem—right then. That's another important lesson: *Focus on the solution, not the problem!*

It's odd, but in retrospect, I think having a near wipeout made me a better businessman and certainly a better entrepreneur. I really had to think in out-of-the-box ways to keep from being buried alive. I also relied on something I'd like to discuss here: positive thinking. Believe me, it works. It got me to where I am today—which is far richer and more successful than I was before the reversal started for me in the 1990s.

Did I ever think I'd be in the *Guinness Book of World Records?* No. I am, though, because of this reversal. It's a fact I'm proud of. Adversity works that way sometimes. Let it work to your advantage.

COACH TRUMP
MAKE IT HAPPEN IN YOUR LIFE

A lot of success depends on how well you can handle pressure. It may seem like a hard fact of life, and it is, but there is something you can do about it. Envision yourself as victorious. Focus on that instead of your nagging doubts and fears. Focus on objective insights and solutions. Pressure can diminish and disappear when you clobber it with a positive attitude. Even if you don't feel indomitable, act that way for a while. It helps!

2

FAILURE IS NOT PERMANENT

Wholeness and the Art of the Comeback

I feel strongly about the importance of *wholeness*. It's a combination of all the components of life that make us healthy, happy, and productive. To my mind, the opposite of wholeness is failure. If it happens, and sometimes it does, the best remedy is to move forward, to realize that failure is not *permanent*, and to immediately focus in the right direction. Ultimately, a solution will show up.

I don't mean to sound like a faith healer, but there is something profound and yet simple about viewing failure as a lack of wholeness. I will also add, it's *effective*. Believing that a negative situation is temporary and wrong will give you the impetus to

5

do something about it, to feel righteous and energetic about fixing it. Being unhappy and unproductive is simply not part of my game plan, and it shouldn't be part of yours, either. See a situation as unacceptable, as taking you away from wholeness, and you will be motivated to get out of it as quickly as possible.

When I had a financial setback in the early 1990s, I saw it more as an aberration from the norm than as a final sentence. I knew what it was like to be whole, and all I had to do was get back to that place. I felt that a comeback was what was expected of me, and I expected it of myself. All I had to do was take the next step and get my momentum going again, which is what I did. It didn't happen overnight, but eventually things started to sort themselves out.

I've seen some people get completely swallowed up by failures. The worst thing you can do to yourself is to believe that bad luck is your due. It isn't! It's not just intelligence or luck that gets us places, it's tenacity in the face of adversity. Some people see problems as bad luck, but I don't. Problems are a part of life and a big part of business. The bigger your business, the bigger your life, the bigger your problems are likely to be. Being prepared for that will save you a lot of emotional turmoil, unnecessary deliberating, and even illness.

I've known people who have come back not just from adversity but from tragedy. There's adversity and then there's tragedy. Thinking about both is a good way to get an objective view of what you may think your problems are. Your situation may be tough, but you can bet others have had far worse things to deal with. One way to pave your way for a comeback (or for a first victory) is to read about people who have been courageous against long odds. My guess is they felt they had an obligation to succeed, and in some cases, an obligation to survive. That's how I feel. I had the privilege of a great family and a great education, and I am serious about honoring those privileges—which means expecting the best from myself.

6

You can have the same attitude, no matter what your situation or background. When failure comes your way, you must believe that you matter, that you can overcome it, and most importantly, that success is what is expected of you. You'd be surprised at what you can accomplish when that's your attitude. It's not just survival, it's not just success, it is your obligation. A sense of duty toward wholeness will go a long way toward your personal and professional success.

What I learned at the time of my worst financial problems is that I was resilient and that I had this indomitable sense of success that couldn't be taken from me no matter what the newspapers said. That brings me to another level of thought, which is faith. Faith is a bit like wisdom. People can help you along the way with it but above all you have to develop it yourself. Faith in yourself can prove to be a very powerful force. Work on it daily. Sometimes when you're fighting a lonely battle, keeping yourself company with positive reinforcement and faith in yourself can be the invisible power that separates the winners from the losers. Losers give up.

In summary: Strive for wholeness, believe in yourself, keep your momentum at full throttle, and be strong and tough in your resilience. Don't expect anything less than that from yourself, and I can assure you that success will become a permanent situation for you, even when your external circumstances may not show it.

Never Give Up!

3

THE APPRENTICE WAS
SUPPOSED TO BE A
BIG MISTAKE

Get the Best Advice You Can,
Then Trust Your Gut

When reality shows hit the scene a few years back, I found the premise interesting but I definitely wasn't interested in doing one. Even when I had been approached multiple times to do a show, I found the ideas boring and stupid. To have cameras following me around, to watch me brush my teeth, comb my hair, conduct meetings, and eat lunch at my desk seemed like an unnecessary interference. I turned them all down without a second thought.

Then a couple of years later, I was asked by Les Moonves, the head of CBS Entertainment, for permission to film the live finale of *Survivor* at Wollman Rink in Central Park. (After I renovated Wollman Rink, I took control through a long-term lease.) I thought it sounded like an interesting idea, so I said yes. When I arrived to see the skating rink transformed into a jungle, I have to admit I was surprised. Then suddenly a young man appeared and introduced himself to me. It was Mark Burnett, and I told him I knew who he was so the introductions weren't necessary. Mark quickly went on to ask me for a meeting to discuss a new idea he had. I said fine.

About a week later, he came to my office, and after some preliminary chat, told me he had an idea for a new jungle reality show, only the jungle would be the canyons of New York City and the world of big business. There would be a 13-week job interview, and the winner would become my apprentice in real life—they would get a job at the Trump Organization. There would also be an educational subtext, which appealed to me immediately. A reality show with some substance could be a new concept for everyone. I told Mark I was interested.

Then what we had to do was pitch the project to the top networks. Everyone wanted it, and they too loved the concept. We went with NBC, who also broadcasts my *Miss Universe, Miss USA*, and *Miss Teen USA* pageants; we already had a strong relationship, so that was a done deal.

Now for some of the challenges. First, not one single person except Mark Burnett and NBC was enthusiastic about *The Apprentice* and my participation in it. All my advisors thought it was a risk, that it would bomb, that my credibility as a businessman would be jeopardized, that my focus would be lost, and that I was making a huge and ultimately very public mistake. When I look back, it's pretty amazing how dead set against it they were. "The biggest mistake you'll ever make" was a common phrase I heard. I didn't feel a lot of support. I reviewed their considerations and thought, I hope they're not right because I already told Mark Burnett I was going to do it. My gut instinct told me it was the right thing to do, without consulting anybody.

The next problem was that Mark Burnett told me that the most time they would need from me each week to film the show was three hours. Three hours for a prime time show! Amazingly, I believed him. When it turned into more like 30 hours, I had some concerns, namely, I was running a huge organization, and already worked about 12 hours a day. How would I handle this? For once, I thought I'd probably overextended myself, big time.

What I decided to do was to take it week by week, realizing it would probably need more time initially and that I could live with that for a short time. What happened is that it gradually did become part of my daily routine, but my days were definitely longer. I adjusted, everyone adjusted, and it gave me a new form of energy as well. If you are faced with a situation that is demanding of your time, give it a chance to settle in. You'll be surprised at how much you can actually do each day.

THE LOW POINT

The week before *The Apprentice* aired for the first time, in January 2004, I remember wondering if that would be the last week of my well-respected life. I couldn't help but think that, considering all the negative advice I'd been given, although the electric energy we seemed to capture during the shooting was strong. Was it just because it was something new for me? Was it really going to be good? What if it was a disaster? How long would it take to recover? There was a huge amount of media attention already. Having a show bomb in that environment wouldn't be easy to handle. These predebut thoughts were the low point for me because they were justified concerns, not just nerves or negativity. What got me through was remembering my gut instinct that said, "This is a great idea—go for it!"

Fortunately, the show was a sensation. It became the number one show very quickly. Everyone was excited about it and so was I—but I was also relieved. It was a big chance to take. It's one thing if you're not well known and your show tanks, but if you're already famous, the sting is worse. If I hadn't decided to take the risk, go against my advisors, and do the show, none of this would have happened. One side effect is that my brand became far better known around the whole world, and there was an amazing media interest in everything I did. That's another form of free advertising. It worked to my benefit as a business-man as well. So when I advise you to take risks, there's a reason for it.

COACH TRUMP
MAKE IT HAPPEN IN YOUR LIFE

I often tell people that I listen to everyone, but the decision will ultimately be mine. That's a good way to be in life and in business. Listen to others, but never negate your own instincts. If I'd listened to everyone, *The Apprentice* would have never happened. We've had six great seasons, and we're getting ready to tape the seventh now. It continues to be a tremendous experience for me and for everyone involved. Not bad for a big mistake! However, when you do take risks, since they won't always work out, you better make sure the upside is big.

4

IS THIS A BLIP OR A CATASTROPHE?

Be Prepared for Things That Happen Outside Your Game Plan

THE SECOND-TALLEST BUILDING IN NORTH AMERICA

W e've all heard of the *Chicago Sun-Times*. What you might not know is that they had the best site in the city, right on the river at North Wabash, next to the landmark Wrigley Building. I wanted it for my Trump International Hotel & Tower/Chicago, and I got it. It's a fantastic location, and if you visit Chicago and take the architectural boat tour of the city, you will see what I mean. When the building comes into sight,

Trump International Hotel & Tower Chicago

it can take your breath away, and that's whether it's windy or not—even though it's only partially finished and won't be completed until 2009. Because of the fantastic asymmetrical shape, the building dominates the view from the Michigan Avenue Bridge and nearby West Wacker Drive. If you visit it, you'll see why we've spent so much time and effort on this building.

My plan for the Chicago building began in 2000, and it was announced that it would be the world's tallest building. I was very excited about this prospect and knew I could get it done, and get it done brilliantly. However, after the terrorist attacks of September 11, 2001, I had the plans scaled down. Much as I wanted to build the tallest building, I don't think making a building a potential target is a smart idea. So we changed the plan a bit.

That was the beginning of a few changes, in fact. We had Skidmore, Owings & Merrill as the building's architect, and they built over 50 models before we decided on something we all liked. Then this design was further refined after comments from the Department of Planning, community groups, and architectural critics of Chicago, who were a big consideration. The revisions were done in 2002, and it was approved. Later, in 2004 we changed 10 floors from offices into hotel rooms and condominiums, based on marketing considerations. We finally began construction on March 17, 2005, five years after I announced the project. You can see by the time line that things don't happen overnight, even if your name is Donald Trump.

This building will be a big beauty. It will be 2.7 million square feet, 92 stories, and will incorporate a health club and spa, a five-star luxury hotel, condominiums, executive lounges, retail shops, and garages. The penthouses will occupy the three top floors. It will be the tallest concrete structure and the second tallest building in North America (after the Sears Tower). The hotel is slated to open in December 2007, with the entire building to be finished by the spring of 2009. The cost will be around $800 million. This is a huge project.

THE LOW POINT

There have been some problems—some big ones, naturally.
Three months after we began foundation construction, we discovered that water had begun leaking into the building site from
the Chicago River. Since the foundation was being laid below the
level of the river, it was always a possibility that the old river
bulkhead that was already in place wouldn't hold. However, that
wasn't the problem—water was coming in through a corner where
the bulkhead and the Wabash Avenue Bridge meet. This could be
a serious problem—so we dealt with it seriously, and it was taken
care of. After a while, it is possible to take problems in stride—if
you have the right attitude and know what you are doing.

Another element of the building that took an odd turn was
the structural design. In the original concept, the base and first
14 floors of the building were designed to be a structural steel
frame, with a reinforced concrete building above. Very late in
the design process, as we were bidding the work, we found that
there was a huge spike in the world commodity prices for steel
due to industrial growth in China absorbing so much of the
world's supply. We went back to the drawing board and
redesigned the building as all concrete, saving several million
dollars in the process and simplifying the construction logistics.

We also had to consider that the rock caissons (supports) for
the tower, which are sunk into the bedrock, make a lot of noise
during construction and we hoped that our Chicago neighbors
could put up with 241 of them being pounded into the bedrock.
About a fourth of the supports had to go down 110 feet into the
limestone, so you can see that this alone was a tremendous project. We got it done and didn't make too many enemies in the
process. Because each of the columns carries 14 million pounds,
the support system has to be carefully and meticulously thought
out and implemented.

We had another problem much earlier in the game when we lost our partner, Conrad Black and the *Chicago Sun-Times*, to a corporate scandal and indictment (and I hope he hangs tough, he's been through a lot). We made a deal to buy out their interest in the project. More recently, we lost our architect at Skidmore, Owings & Merrill when he resigned from the company. These can be big losses, but you know what? We just dealt with them and kept moving forward. We are prepared for problems along the way, and like good soldiers we just keep on going. As the general, I have to admit and take responsibility for the fact that things work out as they will, no matter how prepared you are, but we still do our best to plan and focus—then have the resiliency to immediately regroup from setbacks. Our plans and our resolve were strong enough to continue our work without giving in to any interruptions.

There are bright sides to things, too. For example, we saved over a million dollars by reusing the old river bulkhead from the *Sun-Times* building. We were pleasantly surprised to discover that we had less site cleanup because the newspaper had switched to soy-based ink from petroleum-based ink back in the 1970s, so there was much less ground pollution than we had expected. Sometimes when you start thinking about all the problems you've got, it's a good idea to focus a little on some of the positives in the situation.

COACH TRUMP
MAKE IT HAPPEN IN YOUR LIFE

When things happen that might be outside the outline of your game plan, ask yourself, "Is this a blip or is it a catastrophe?" We had some blips along the way with our Chicago building, and we'll probably have a couple more, but it's still been a fantastic development and experience. Will you have problems when you tackle something big? Yes. Will you let them derail you? You absolutely should not.

Let your passion for your work carry you through all the setbacks they can throw at you. Be it wind, water, resignations, scandals, whatever—you can prevail. Your insurance for overcoming these perils is free—it's called *never giving up!*

After a while, it is possible to take problems in stride—if you have the right attitude and know what you are doing. Have the resilience to immediately regroup and change course if you need to after you hit a setback.

5

I LOVE A GOOD FIGHT

The Trump SoHo Hotel Condominium

SoHo has been a chic neighborhood for some years now, and I waited a long time to enter it as a developer. I knew it'd be a fight to get anything going there because most of SoHo is made up of low-rise buildings and is subject to strict zoning laws. I doubt if any of you would think of or refer to SoHo as a manufacturing center, but for historical reasons, that's how much of it is zoned. So, building a residential structure in the locations I wanted is not permitted. However, you can build a hotel there. When I learned that, I decided to build a condominium hotel in SoHo—a tall one.

SoHo is considered a mecca for art, film, and fashion buffs, with over 250 art galleries, 100 designer stores, and over 200 restaurants. In other words, it's a great area to visit and an even greater area to stay. I believed SoHo deserved—and was ready for—a first-rate, twenty-first-century hotel.

The 45-story, $450 million tower I hoped to build with my partners, Bayrock Group and the Sapir Organization, was, of course, met with a fury of opposition from local community activists and the politicians that represent them. I wouldn't let that stop us. I announced my intention on June 6, 2006, on *The Apprentice*. Despite everything that ensued, on May 8, 2007, I'm pleased to report, we were approved by city officials to erect this condo hotel. Along the way, we had a few problems to deal with, which was not a huge surprise.

The biggest obstacle was the height of the building. SoHo is a low-rise neighborhood, and this project would significantly alter the skyline. It would be the tallest building between midtown and the financial district. It's not that SoHo isn't zoned for tall buildings—it is—but none have ever been built. We wanted to change that. There were "air rights" laws—the right to build higher—already in place that made it perfectly legal to

Trump SoHo Hotel Condominium New York

build a high-rise. In fact, we added several floors to the hotel's design by buying the air rights from the neighboring properties.

Although we had the right to build a hotel with the height we wanted, the fact that no one had done it before worked against us. This project was the first time New York City's Department of Buildings had to consider a condominium hotel in one of New York City's manufacturing districts, which do not permit residential use. The City's antiquated zoning laws and the local residents, together, created formidable obstacles.

New York City (unlike many other major U.S. destination cities) had never before been confronted with a hotel comprised entirely of condominiums. The key zoning consideration for the City was that the units would not be residences for the owners, but would be for transient occupancy. That meant we had to prove to the Department of Buildings that Trump SoHo would not be a residential building, but a building for short-term stays—and I firmly believed we could convince the City officials of this.

A condo hotel is not an apartment. It operates on the premise that the buyers have the right to use their condo units for only a certain number of days each year, and when an owner is not occupying their condo hotel unit the units get rented out as hotel rooms. It's a great setup because both the owner and the management company collect revenues. The units in Trump SoHo are not designed for permanent residences, nor would an owner use his or her unit that way (the look, feel, and design of a luxury hotel is far, far different than that of a residential building). We worked tirelessly with the City to make our intentions clear.

As expected, everyone and their cousin came after me for this, and the Greenwich Village Society for Historical Preservation called my plan a "Trojan horse" way to sneak condos into manufacturing districts across the City. They said my motives were entirely covert. How a 45-story building can be considered a covert operation is beyond me, but you get the idea. There were demonstrations and neighborhood alliances that made it clear that I would not be receiving a warm welcome. So what else is new? Meanwhile, the silent majority of the neighborhood actually supported the project and saw it for what it is: a major attraction for tourism and business. The project will significantly improve a neighborhood that had been artificially suppressed for years as a result of its antiquated manufacturing zoning.

Despite the very vocal minority, I wasn't about to be slowed down. We started excavation in 2006 even though we had not yet received approval to build above ground.

Then another problem arose.

In December, the excavating contractors came across some human remains that were later determined to be about a century old. We immediately and voluntarily halted work. The police arrived, and the city ordered us to stop work on the lot altogether. This may not have been legal, but we agreed. We then hired a team of archeologists to excavate and identify the remains. At this point, what we didn't need was more publicity while waiting for approval, but of course it made the news, and one director of a city preservation society quipped that we should rename the project Trump Condo Hotel & Mausoleum. It's always something, isn't it? In the end and despite all of the hoopla in the press, by attacking the skeleton problem immediately and in force we were able to get back to work within a week.

Then the bloggers got going on the subject of the hotel and the discovery, and it was a big topic for a while. We were also getting many letters from citizens and societies opposing our constructing the building. There were demonstrations at the site, and the controversy went on for close to a year. Additionally, we were accused of building a 45-story target for a terrorist attack, and there was an online cartoon that had a skeleton with a comb-over as an advertisement for the new building. One thing for certain is that all of New York and all New Yorkers knew I was building a new building. Someone once said I was a great promoter, but sometimes I don't have to do a thing to get attention.

The hits kept coming, and it felt like being in the eye of the hurricane, but it made us solid and stronger in our mission. At one point, someone got hold of some of our early drafts of marketing materials mentioning that the units would be a great residential opportunity—which created a political and activist firestorm. However, we stayed focused on what we wanted: to get approval. We knew we couldn't change the zoning nor could we build under the existing zoning if the building was characterized as residential. So we were very focused on proving to the City that the building was not residential and that we could proceed within the existing zoning laws.

We showed the City that we had specific constraints regarding occupancy that were very clear. My team ended up negotiating with the City for months over a six-page "Restrictive Declaration," which included many hour-long sessions where the City officials would analyze and critique every comma in that document (literally). We were airtight and transparent in what was being offered. Our condo plan published everything in black and white. Nothing was hidden. As a result, we finally got approval—our proposed building was absolutely within the zoning laws of SoHo, and no one could argue otherwise. My father had always said, "Know everything you can about what you're doing," and that's the advice I followed. Every adversity served as fuel in what had become a fight of city-sized proportions.

As of today, the Trump SoHo project is going along beautifully. Both Don Jr. and Ivanka are working on it with me and my partners, as did Sean Yazbeck, *The Apprentice* season five winner, and Julius Schwarz of Bayrock.

It's going to be a wonderful, elegant, and tasteful addition to the SoHo neighborhood. There will be 25,000 square feet of commercial space that will include a top-notch restaurant, a 7,500-square-foot spa, and a 12,000-square-foot conference center, and there will be 360-degree views from the 12th floor up. We'll have a stunning year-round pool with full-service private cabanas, a private library, a café, bar, and restaurant, and I can guarantee you that my SoHo neighbors are going to love it—eventually. It will enhance their property value, for one thing, because it's going to be a beauty. Be sure to visit the famous manufacturing district of SoHo when you come to New York and take a look.

SoHo caused perhaps a few more problems than expected, but it was all in a year's work—to us. That's big city business and we are big enough to handle it. Be sure you have the same attitude—it will save you a lot of unnecessary anxiety.

COACH TRUMP
MAKE IT HAPPEN IN YOUR LIFE

Adversity is a fact of life. Chances are that you will never wake up to an adversity-free day. Accept this as a challenge—rather than a disappointment. Be bigger than the problems, be ready to fight for your rights, and all will be well.

6

REMEMBERING
SEPTEMBER 11, 2001

If You Never Give Up, You'll Be Able to Give Back

I was watching the morning news on television in my apartment on September 11, 2001, when I first saw what had happened. The rest I could see from my window. I had predicted an attack in my book *The America We Deserve*, which was published in 2000, but that doesn't mean I wasn't affected by what happened that day. It was an act of depravity and spiritual destitution. After the attacks, some people and companies left New York City but I never considered moving. I'm a New Yorker and this is my home. I knew that New Yorkers are resilient and that New York City would not only survive, but thrive, which has happened.

Since then, the Trump Organization has always had an annual memorial of some sort on September 11. The first year, we forfeited our annual Trump Organization Christmas party in order to give the funds that would normally be used for that event to charity. All of us felt it was the right thing to do, and it was. Since then, we have had a memorial in the lobby and atrium of Trump Tower each year, and I attend as do other members of the Trump Organization.

In 2006 and 2007, we had the September Concert perform at Trump Tower on 9/11, and it was open to the public. The September Concert was founded in 2002 on the first anniversary of 9/11 with the message of peace through music. Haruko Smith, the founder, and Veronica Kelly, the vice chairman, have done an amazing job. My son Eric introduces the concert, and all of us attend. It's a meaningful celebration and a positive response to a day that shouldn't be forgotten.

It takes time for us to help coordinate this event and to make the space available in our very busy building, but it is worth every minute of it. That's just one example of why it pays to never give up—you'll eventually be in a position to give back.

I host many charity events at my golf courses and have the annual Red Cross Ball at my Mar-a-Lago Club in Palm Beach. These events don't just happen—they require a lot of planning and that means time and effort, not to mention money. Owning properties is a lot more than just ownership—it's about making them useful. If you plan to go into real estate just to make money or to feel powerful, that's not enough. If you can see your gains as a way to share, you will find your work will be much more rewarding—and probably more profitable in the long run.

Every year we host the Salvation Army in our lobby to kick off the holiday season. This has become a tradition. A band plays, the media is there, I give a brief speech, and the Salvation Army gets some of the recognition it deserves for the great job they've been doing for so many years. This too takes a lot of time to arrange, but we do it every year.

Sometimes being a giver will open you up to new talents. Each year I donate an autographed doodle to the Doodle for Hunger auction at Tavern on the Green. It's a great event, and contributors have included Sting, Muhammad Ali, Larry King, Al Pacino, Billy Joel, Valentino, Bill Cosby, Paul McCartney, Kirk Douglas, Martina Navratilova, Peter Max, Bette Midler, Jack Nicklaus, Cindy Crawford, and many other distinguished people. It takes me a few minutes to draw something, in my case, it's usually a building or a cityscape of skyscrapers, and then sign my name, but it raises thousands of dollars to help the hungry in New York through the Capuchin Food Pantries Ministry. The auction was an innovative idea that has helped many people, and I don't mind spending a little time for a very good cause. Art may not be my strong point, but the end result is help for people who need it.

Doodle for Hunger

I can remember a friend who asked me why I had so many charity events at my properties. He seemed perplexed that I would do this, because it wasn't really necessary, and he knew how much time it required. I said to him, "Because I can." Believe me, those are powerful words, with an equally powerful feeling to go along with them. Imagine saying that to someone yourself—"Because I can!" It's a great feeling, and it makes all the work that went into acquiring and developing those beautiful properties and buildings worth it.

We've all seen bad situations that we'd like to be able to help. Being successful allows you to help in a big way. That's another reason to keep at it. Knowing you're going to be able to give back more if you succeed is a wonderful incentive to keep going. If you never give up, you'll be able to give back—and that's something to remember.

7

EXPECT PROBLEMS AND
YOU'LL BE READY WHEN
THEY COME

Getting Trump Tower Off the Ground

Trump Tower was my first huge success, and I will always love this building. It makes me feel great that it's now the number three tourist destination in New York City. Trump Tower has been famous for so long that most people think it's just always been here, or that it just appeared one day on the midtown skyline of New York City. I can tell you that is not the case. In fact, people are always surprised to hear that I almost named it Tiffany Tower, and there are many other background incidents that made the construction of this landmark building particularly challenging. If you think putting up this tower was a magical occurrence, even for a developer like me, you've got

Trump Tower

some interesting reading ahead of you—especially if you enjoy labyrinthine stories.

Robert Moses, a great figure in the history of New York City, said something that stayed with me the entire time I was attempting to get Trump Tower started and finished: *"You can't make an omelet without breaking eggs."* Sometimes I felt like changing it to say, *"You can't build a skyscraper without breaking a few heads."*

Nothing was easy from day one. To begin the saga, it took me almost three years to even get a response from the man who controlled the land I wanted to buy. I made calls and wrote letter after letter. I learned a lot about persistence, but I also learned that if you are passionate about something, receiving zero encouragement still won't discourage you. I just plain wouldn't give up. When the site eventually became available, I realized that my letters had helped.

The site where I wanted to build Trump Tower was adjacent to Tiffany's. Further down the line, I needed to convince Tiffany's to let me buy their air rights—their right to build a tall skyscraper on top of their store—for $5 million. That would prevent anyone from being able to rip down the Tiffany's building and put up a tower that would block my views. I would be able to build a tower with soaring picture windows versus tiny ones, an aesthetic consideration that was of utmost importance.

In order to get the zoning variance I needed from the City of New York, I had to know whether I'd have the air rights. The man in charge of this told me he liked my idea and my price, but that he was going on vacation for a month and would get back to me. In a month's time, I would have done a lot of zoning work as well as architectural work, and if I wasn't sure of getting the air rights, I would be wasting a lot of time and work. Fortunately for me, I was dealing with a real gentleman, Walter Hoving, and he told me that his word was good. Period. In fact, he seemed insulted that I would question his decision and his word. Once in awhile, but not often, you run into someone as honorable as that.

Now that I had Tiffany's air rights, I needed one more parcel, which was a tiny site along 57th Street adjacent to Tiffany's. This was required by another New York City zoning regulation: You have to have a minimum of 30 feet of open space, like a rear yard, behind any building. Without this piece of property, I would have had to cut the rear yard out of the building we'd already designed.

It turned out that this piece of property was owned by Leonard Kandell, who was as honorable as Walter Hoving. However, he didn't want to part with his land. He wasn't a seller, and he wouldn't budge. Until one day I found a bonus in the paperwork for my Tiffany deal. It included a clause that gave Tiffany an option to buy the Kandell property within a certain time frame because it was adjacent to Tiffany. Maybe something could be worked out with Kandell after all.

By now I realized what I was trying to do was never going to be easy. Every door required a lot of work just to get it cracked open to begin with. Robert Moses' quote would surface again in my mind and I would just keep going. It helps to expect problems because then, in a sense, you're ready for them and not thrown off balance. It's good to remind yourself of that—daily, if necessary.

So then, I had to go back to Walter Hoving and ask him if I could buy his option on Leonard Kandell's property as part of my deal with Tiffany's. I knew he had no interest in buying Kandell's property anyway. Walter agreed. However, Leonard said the option belonged to Tiffany and was not transferable. He might have been right. It was also possible that if I sued over this question, I might win the right to exercise the option.

So I explained the possibility of litigation to Leonard, and in less than half an hour, we managed to make a deal that was good for both of us: I would withdraw my exercise of the option, and Leonard would agree to extend my lease on his site from 20 years to 100 years, which was enough time to make it financeable. Also in the lease, he eliminated any prohibitions against rezoning. Leonard and I remained friends, and I was allowed to continue on my quest to build Trump Tower.

I still didn't have a final contract with Genesco, the company that owned Bonwit Teller, the store that was sitting on the property where I wanted to build Trump Tower. We'd managed to keep the whole deal completely secret and were expecting to sign contracts in a couple of months. Word began to leak out and suddenly Genesco was inundated with interested buyers, among them Arab investors with oil money. Not surprisingly, Genesco began to try to get out of the deal.

However, I had fortunately gotten a one-page letter of intent from Jack Hanigan, who had been brought in by Genesco to save them when they were having difficulties. He had been receiving those letters I'd been writing for three years. I let Genesco know that I would litigate and hold up the sale of the Bonwit property for years if they didn't honor our deal. I wasn't even sure if the letter would be legally binding, but I could prove to be a nuisance to them if they reneged.

Shortly after this, I got a call from the *New York Times* who had heard that I was about to make a deal with Genesco to buy the Bonwit building. We had kept this quiet but I realized I should take a risk, especially considering that Genesco was faltering on their side of the deal. So I told the reporter that we'd reached an agreement, and I was planning on building a new tower on the Bonwit site. Therefore, the store would be closed, most likely, in a few months.

The article appeared the next morning, and I was hoping it would put some pressure on Genesco. What happened is something I hadn't counted on—as soon as the article appeared, all of Bonwit's employees went over to Bergdorf Goodman, Saks Fifth Avenue, and Bloomingdale's to hunt for new jobs, and as a result, Bonwit was having trouble running their store. Five days later, I had the contract signed with Genesco.

We hadn't even gotten close to construction yet. This is a good example of the perseverance you need and some of the obstacles that can arise when you are trying to do something great. Sometimes it's hard even when you're trying to do something far smaller than a skyscraper. For those of you who think I have the Midas touch and everything comes easily, just remember some of these episodes when you confront your own problems along the way to success. Because believe me, you will have problems! It doesn't matter if your name is Trump or not, we all experience these things. Expect it! When I look back, it was a wonderful, exhilarating experience and every difficult moment was worth it.

8

FREQUENTLY ASKED
QUESTIONS

I get a ton of fan mail these days, and a large percentage of it is from people asking for advice. Sometimes entire classrooms will send me their questions. I've decided to include a few of these questions with my responses.

1. How do you handle the person who consistently makes the same mistakes over and over?

   I don't. They're working for someone else now.

2. What is the most important characteristic of a good leader?

   Discipline. It helps if everyone has it, but if a leader doesn't, he or she won't be one for very long.

3. What are the most important steps for someone who intends to be successful?

Do your homework. In other words, learn everything you can about what you want, know what you are up against, and research every aspect of your endeavor. Talk to all the experts you can find. It can't be a hit or miss approach. The odds are already against you, so don't make it harder on yourself by being negligent.

4. What will distinguish the leaders of tomorrow in the real estate industry?

   Those who have both vision and discipline will succeed. One is useless without the other. With both, you have a chance of becoming a leader, provided you've learned and sharpened your instincts through your experiences.

5. Who are some of the people in history you admire, and why?

   Abraham Lincoln is one, because he was president at the most difficult time in our country's history. He was also self-educated and endured many years of adversity prior to becoming president. Another would be Winston Churchill, a leader at a pivotal time in world history—World War II. He was a great orator who inspired thousands of people with his speeches, and he won the Nobel Prize in literature for his historical writing.

6. What is your favorite dessert?

   Ice cream.

7. What do you like about your job?

   Everything. Every day is a challenge, and every day is great.

8. Do you go out for lunch?

   Very rarely. I don't like breaking up my work day. It interferes with my momentum. I prefer to have something to eat at my desk, which takes maybe 5 or 10 minutes.

9. What advice do you have for someone who wants to start his own business?

Be ready for problems—you'll have them every day. Keep your focus no matter what and be as big as your daily challenges. Never give up!

10. What if things don't work out the way we want, even if we work really hard?

First of all, know that you've got a lot of company. I've waited 30 years to see some things happen. Some people have waited longer. Always consider that it's possible you might be doing the wrong thing, so that no matter how hard you work, it's just not going to happen. Make sure you're doing what is right for you. You have to love doing it. Then be tenacious.

11. Do you believe in luck?

Yes. I know I'm lucky. I was also fortunate to have a great role model. I worked around my father from an early age and learned a lot from him.

12. What did you want to be when you were a kid?

I wanted to be either a baseball player or a builder. I liked to build skyscrapers with my building blocks. I was a good enough baseball player to be offered scholarships and had also considered going to USC to study film, but my knowledge of and love for real estate led me to Wharton.

13. Where do you get your ideas?

The world inspires me, and keeping up with world events can give you a lot of ideas. In this age of technology, we have access to more and more information at a faster pace than ever before, and I find that exciting. I keep an open mind and that's a good way for ideas to start happening.

14. Do you ever fear that you might fail at something?

    I have a pretty good track record of successes by now, but failure is always a possibility. I am cautious but not fearful. There's a difference. It's important to be circumspect—know that the possibility of success is there as well as failure. Risk plays a part in everything we do. I could get hit by a bus while I am crossing the street. Things happen. Don't let fear interfere with your plans.

15. What do you do on your vacations?

    I don't take vacations in the sense of planning a trip somewhere and then going there to rest. I find my work energizing and never feel a need to get away from it. Since I own golf courses and love to golf, I can have a great time golfing while inspecting the course. In the winter I go down to my Mar-a-Lago Club in Palm Beach on the weekends, so I can golf year round. I take weekends more than vacations, which works for me.

16. We like your show, *The Apprentice*. We were wondering if you like firing people.

    I don't like firing anyone. Sometimes it's necessary, but I'd rather keep people around me for a long time. I have employees who have been with me for over 30 years. The best working environment is when everyone has the same work ethic and focus and does their best. That's the case with most of my employees, but not always, and if not then a change has to be made.

17. When you first started out in real estate, what was your main goal?

    I wanted to be successful on my own terms. My father had been successful in real estate, and I wanted to succeed on my own. I'd always loved beautiful buildings and

Manhattan, so my focus was there. I wanted to follow my own vision, and I did.

18. What was the most surprising thing about *The Apprentice* to you?

    My image changed. I became very popular after I started firing people every week!

19. What makes you happiest?

    That's a complex question for being so simple. I'd say several things make me happy: Doing well. Doing my best. Doing a great job and knowing it's great. Being able to share that accomplishment is good, too—I can increase the value of neighborhoods and communities, provide jobs, and I'm in a position to give back in charitable ways. My family is very important to me and always has been. I'm happiest when I'm with them.

20. What was your favorite subject in school?

    I liked anything to do with mathematics. I excelled in geometry.

21. What is your favorite movie?

    Citizen Kane.

22. What time do you get up in the morning?

    Five a.m.

23. What's the best thing about being rich?

    Being able to give back is a great feeling.

24. What's the best piece of advice you can give me?

    Never give up. You can accomplish more things with that attitude than anything else I can tell you.

9

WHEN THE OTHER SIDE
EXPECTS A DUEL, OFFER
A PARTNERSHIP

*Trump International Golf
Links, Scotland*

I have always been interested in building a golf course in Scotland for two very good reasons aside from the spectacular beauty of that country: My mother was born there, and Scotland is the birthplace of golf. Golf has been an important part of my life, and needless to say, so was my mother.

I spent five years reviewing sites and I turned down over 200 possibilities for development throughout Europe. I was waiting patiently for the right place, and when I saw the links land at Menie Estate, which is in northeast Scotland's Grampian

Trump Scotland Golfing

Region, I knew it was the right place. Menie Estate and Menie House, which dates from the fourteenth century, is 12 miles north of Aberdeen, which is Scotland's third largest city. More important, I had never seen such a dramatic unspoiled seaside landscape. It contained sand dunes of immense proportions, three miles of spectacular oceanfront, and 1400 acres in all. It was stunning, and I got excited.

THE LOW POINT: IT'S NOT EASY WHEN PEOPLE LAUGH IN YOUR FACE

I knew that Scotland had a reputation for being a great place when it came to development and business, so I was enthusiastic to begin work there. However, the announcement of my proposed development caused some consternation and the environmentalists were immediately on guard. In fact, I remember people openly laughing when they saw the scope of what I had planned. This site is of environmental and historical significance to Scotland, and no one thought I would get approvals to go ahead. The environmental statement on Menie Estate alone takes up two five-inch-thick books.

The main problem centered around an environmental concern I had never encountered before called geomorphology. It was brought to our attention by our environmental experts and by the Scottish National Heritage Organization. Since addressing this subject was a Planning Board requirement and a major hurdle, we took it very seriously and tried to learn everything we could. We hired the leading authority on geomorphology, and every detail was seriously considered. I think we surprised everyone by our concern and professional conscience, and our perseverance and integrity was noted by the decision makers involved.

Back to geomorphology, which is the study of movement landforms, including their origin and evolution and the processes that have shaped them over the years. The remarkable sand dunes found on the Menie Estate are a restricted area comprising a total of 25 acres of land. They move by natural forces—which can spell disaster for a golf course. We looked at maps from many years ago and saw how the entire 25 acres of dunes had literally moved to a different location by nature's force, and so we knew the environmental concerns and ours were valid.

We did extensive research on this problem and discovered the dunes could be stabilized by planting beds of marram grass, whose root system allows it to thrive in windswept and harsh climates. This grass protects the sand dunes and also adds another dimension of natural beauty to the landscape.

In addition, based on our environmental research, we made many other recommendations to improve and protect the local wildlife: The creation of three artificial holts for otters and a written otter protection plan; preparation of a badger protection plan, based on new surveys; new habitat creation for Red List breeding birds; erection of nest boxes and bat boxes at Menie House; biodiversity target actions to maintain and enhance the Palmate Newt, Black-Headed Gulls and wading birds, Brown Hare, and Wych Elm; and creation of new slacks, plant and habitat translocation, and seed collection to maintain young dune slack habitat. And that's just a partial list. Remember when I mentioned the two five-inch-thick books? I wasn't exaggerating. So if you think things just happen because my name is Donald Trump, let this be a reminder that it doesn't work that way.

When we finally submitted the final outline of the planning application to the Aberdeenshire Council, it addressed both the environmental and business issues of the development. On the economic side, the construction project would create approximately 6,230 jobs in Aberdeenshire and 740 jobs in the rest of Scotland. The ongoing operation would support a total of 1,250 jobs and 1,440 long-term jobs. Overall, the project could create as much as 205 million pounds in economic value for Aberdeenshire and 262 million pounds for Scotland. Those are some of the facts and figures we submitted, and as you can see, our research had to be very detailed. It's no surprise that support was enthusiastic from the local business community. For my part, this will be an expensive development, costing nearly $1 billion pounds, but it's really a labor of love for me.

As I write this a year after the first big environmental issues surfaced, we are going ahead with our vision with very few impediments. How did it happen? How did we overcome the challenges people thought were insurmountable? People were expecting a duel, and instead, we offered a partnership. We worked with the Scottish National Heritage and forged a partnership based on our collective concerns. We did a huge amount of background work and environmental research that took a lot of time and effort on our part, but it was time well spent. Along the way, we broke the barriers and mistrust by being vigilant, open, and honest, and by hiring the best people to get the job done properly. We offered a superior product, and no one could challenge our credibility.

The fact that we were environmentally sensitive gave the authorities faith in our ability to do what was best for everyone. Being sympathetic to the rich history and heritage of the area and the overall impact our development might have, as it turned out, was not a sacrifice by any means. It will remain an ongoing concern for centuries to come, I would hope. The Scottish National Heritage is doing their job, and so are we.

We are still awaiting approvals for some areas of our development, and George Sorial from the Trump Organization, who I asked to manage the project, has been traveling to Scotland every two or three weeks to oversee progress. I'll be going over in about two weeks, and I've enjoyed every trip I've taken to Scotland. (Coincidentally, George's mother was born and raised on the Isle of Lewis, where my mother grew up.)

Martin Hawtree is designing the course, and we hope to have it done in two years. That's not all—we will have a golf driving range, a golf academy, and a short game practice area. The home of golf deserves this kind of comprehensive attention, and we are designing the course to be the best links golf course on earth. It will be the perfect site to host an Open or the Ryder Cup down the line.

In addition to the golf links, which will eventually include two 18-hole links golf courses, we are building 950 condominiums, 500 houses, a 450-room hotel, 36 golf villas, and accommodations for 400 staff members. This will be a destination point for all golf lovers of the world, and the standard for golf development will reach a new plateau when we are finished. It hasn't been an easy road, but after waiting and looking for five determined years, every bit of work has been worth it. As a result, I'm nearly an expert at geomorphology. Who could ask for anything more?

10

SEPARATE YOURSELF
FROM THE
COMPLAINING CROWD

You Can Create Your Own Luck

You may have heard the saying, "luck is when opportunity meets preparedness." I agree. I've often heard people talking about how so-and-so is so lucky (as if to emphasize that they themselves are *not* lucky). I think what's really happening is the complainers aren't "working themselves into luck." If you want to be lucky, prepare for something big.

Sure, it might be more fun to watch movies but unless you're going into the film industry, it's not the best use of your time. Developing your talents requires work, and work creates luck. Having this attitude toward success is a great way to set yourself on a rewarding course for your life.

There was a lot of talk for a while about venting your frustrations and anxieties and how it might be healthy to get them off your chest. To a point, yes, but to an exaggerated degree, no. I read an article recently about how complaining, without doing anything about it, is actually detrimental to physical and mental well-being. With the advent of blogging and all the other sorts of opinion-gushing venues available to everyone now, people are spending way too much time harping on negative themes. The emphasis is out of balance, and the negative focus doesn't help the situation.

Don't dwell so much on a problem that you've exhausted yourself before you can even entertain a solution. It just doesn't make sense. It takes brainpower and energy to think positively and creatively—and to *see* creatively and positively. Going negative is the easy way, the lazy way. Use your brainpower to focus on positives and solutions, and your own mindset will help create your own luck.

Shakespeare put it this way, in a famous quote from *Julius Caesar:* "The fault is not in our stars, dear Brutus, but in ourselves." That's a clear message. We are responsible for ourselves. We are responsible for our own luck. What an empowering thought! If you see responsibility as a bum deal, then you are not seeing it for what it really is—a great opportunity.

Let's say you're facing some big challenge today. I can tell you right now you've got a lot of company. What will separate you from the complaining crowd will be how you choose to look at your situation. If you believe you are in control of it—and you are—you will know exactly who to look for when you need help: yourself. You could be your greatest discovery yet for success, luck, power, and happiness.

When I encountered enormous financial challenges back in the 1990s, I was mature enough to assume responsibility and know that the problem was mine. I knew it wouldn't do any good to blame other people. That would be a waste of time, and that's one kind of loss I don't like. Time is something that cannot be replaced. If you find yourself slipping into the blaming others mode, get out of it quickly.

Give luck the chance it needs to play itself out in your life. No one can do it for you. As soon as you discover that luck is yours to create, you'll be thinking and seeing things in a whole new way. So work hard, have fun, and good luck.

11

SOMETIMES YOU HAVE TO SWALLOW YOUR PRIDE

Trump International Hotel & Tower, New York

We've all heard of beauty makeovers. Sometimes the results are amazing. I like to do the same thing with buildings. Sometimes it requires more innovation to improve things in a big way than to build something new. The challenges can be more complex which is why a lot of developers are quick to tear down existing structures and start over with a site. I have a few good examples of buildings (and businesses) that were worth salvaging, and they have turned out to be resounding successes. The first thing to keep in mind is that you have

Trump International Hotel & Tower

to be resolved not to give up in the face of more problems than
you might normally encounter.

Trump International Hotel & Tower is located at One Central Park West, a fantastic location with unobstructed views of
the park. It has been rated the #1 hotel in *Travel & Leisure* and

the *New York Post.* What a lot of people don't know is that it was formerly the Gulf & Western/Paramount building. It was owned by General Electric, which had Jack Welch, John Myers, and Dale Frey at the helm; and it was an office building. It really stands out because it's one of the few tall towers on the West Side. It went up in the early 1960s, just before zoning laws were passed that would prohibit such a tall building at that location.

This building managed to attract a lot of attention, not just because of its height, but because of some construction problems that had the tenants on edge. For one thing, it swayed in the wind and would flex at the top with winds of only 15 miles per hour. All buildings have some flexibility but this was an exceptional situation. Elevators would stop, and some tenants even said they felt seasick. Once, when there was a high wind, the upper windows fell out. These episodes were legendary.

Let's just say this building had some problems, some pretty major problems. Also, it was not constructed very well because the outside curtain was made of glass and cheap aluminum, and it was chock full of asbestos. The good news was that the building structure was classic and had wonderfully high ceilings. It was worth saving for those important reasons alone.

When I heard this building was for sale, I called Dale Frey and asked to meet him. That's when I found out he was receiving calls from many major developers around the country. I would have a lot of competition. However, I arranged for a meeting, and I explained that if the building was completely demolished, it could only be rebuilt as a 19-story building versus the 52 fabulous stories that it was. That alone was a big reason to see what could be salvaged, but it would require a lot of research, which I immediately started doing.

What I suggested was that the steel structure could be strengthened, and the high ceilings would be ideal for a residential building, which was also a hotter item in the market than a business space would be. This was the perfect location for a luxury residential building. General Electric seemed impressed with my ideas, and I felt good about their positive reaction to everything I had presented. My only concern at this point was that I was just emerging from some financial problems, so they might be hesitant to take a chance on me.

What happened next came as a shock. Dale Frey called to tell me that while he liked my plans a lot, they were putting the job out to bid. They would ask some of the biggest real estate firms in the country to put in a bid, and he hoped I'd be among them. I was astonished by this because I had spent a lot of time on my concept, and had explained it to them personally. Now I had to start over and bid like a newcomer to the project.

I felt miserable and a bit outraged by this turn of events. I'd basically be entering a public contest, which I didn't think was necessary. I was wondering if they had just been humoring me all that time, even though they appeared to be interested and impressed with my ideas. What could I do? I was definitely interested, I'd already spent a lot of time and effort on this, so I finally swallowed my pride and decided to just go for it. I like challenges and this had become an even bigger one, not that I was happy about it. So I worked on a fantastic and detailed presentation. When I say put everything into what you're doing, this was a good example.

It seemed like ages, but General Electric finally called to say they were going with me. Being chosen by this power group to develop this incredible site was wonderful news. Trump International Hotel & Tower would become a reality. It made all the aggravation of the process worth it. Dale Frey and John Myers at GE made it possible—they are great guys.

In 1995, we began to demolish the former Gulf & Western tower—only the steel structure would remain. I had Philip Johnson lined up as the architect along with Costas Kondylis & Associates, so we were assured of a spectacular as well as elegant building. Philip Johnson had designed the State Theater at Lincoln Center, which is only a few blocks away. This was an

Trump International Globe

important building and I wanted the very best. That's exactly what all of us got.

Trump International Hotel & Tower is now the #1 hotel in New York City. It includes Jean Georges Restaurant, which is acknowledged as one of the great restaurants of the world. The condominiums in the building stay on the market for a very short time. There are waiting lists for everything concerned with this building. It's also the first time a hotel and condominium have been combined, which people now hail as an innovation. It wasn't an innovation to me, just common sense. In fact, it's an idea that is copied around the world today and with great success. So take the time to think things through.

Yes, the original building had major problems; yes, the approval process was confounding, but that was part of the challenge. It also provided me with a great opportunity. Sometimes you have to look a little harder to see those opportunities, but believe me, it's worth it.

12

COURAGE ISN'T THE ABSENCE OF FEAR, IT'S THE CONQUERING OF FEAR

Courage means never giving up. It's much easier to give up, and that's exactly what losers do. Being knocked down is one thing—staying down is another. Some very ordinary people have accomplished remarkable things by simply being persistent and never giving up. Abraham Lincoln is a good example—his courage made him extraordinary.

On *The Apprentice*, the candidates must first go through a grueling audition process. There have been millions of applicants, and only a few people are chosen. Those aren't terrific odds. That's why I firmly believe that there are no losers on that show. The people who try out for the program show great courage to begin with. They are all winners. Being fired in front of millions of people isn't easy, but that's part of the deal and they persist anyway. Most of them say the experience was worth everything they put into it, whether they won or not.

Hemingway wrote the now familiar phrase, "Courage is grace under pressure." Think about it. Some days we are faced with challenges that we'd rather not have to deal with, but we get up and deal with them anyway. That's courage. It requires a certain poise. Maybe it's not heroic, maybe every day isn't going to bring a calamitous situation, but it's an example of bravery that we can all understand.

Self-confidence is a component of courage that we all need. Sometimes we need a push in the right direction. I worked with a young executive who had never done any public speaking, so he decided he wasn't any good at it. He told me so, and I thought to myself, "He hasn't even tried public speaking, and he tells me he's no good at it!" I had a feeling he'd be good at it. A few months later when I realized I wouldn't be able to make a dinner engagement that included a short speech, I told him he'd have to step in for me. He told me, "I don't do public speaking." I said to him, "You do now." End of conversation. Do you know what? He's become an accomplished speaker. Courage isn't the absence of fear, it's the conquering of fear.

The phenomenon of stage fright is a good example. I read an article recently about how common stage fright is, even among professional actors. There are a lot of very accomplished and famous performers who deal with it regularly, sometimes for decades. They don't let their fear get in the way of their passion. I'm used to speaking in front of tens of thousands of people, and I find it enjoyable, but I've often had people ask me if I get nervous. I don't. I just go out and do it.

Winston Churchill was a great orator, but I read that he spent a lot of time developing this skill. He wasn't a natural in the beginning, but he worked at it until he mastered it. He became a powerful and mesmerizing speaker. One of his most famous speeches during World War II included these words:

> Never, never, never, never, never, in nothing great or small, large or petty, never give in, except to convictions of honour and good sense. Never yield to force; never yield to the apparently overwhelming might of the enemy.

Churchill and his people were in danger of being bombed out and overrun by the German military when he said that. You might not be experiencing the blitz, but you can still apply those words of courage to your daily life. There are days when I have so many problems come at me at once that it can seem like the blitz. I don't give in to them, and neither should you—ever!

Another important thing about courage is that it will help you think and act in the right way. It will help you focus on the opportunities in front of you instead of on the problems. Problems are often opportunities coming at us in packaging that isn't what we expect or want. This has happened to me more times than I can count. So when I say I welcome problems, there's a reason for it. Keep your mind flexible and open to creative solutions to your problems. Einstein said, "You can't solve a problem with the same thinking that created the problem." That's a good way to avoid brain cramps as well as find a solution.

Back to courage. Remember that fear can be conquered. Know that you are capable of courage and that you are designed to succeed—that's half the battle. Then go full throttle, and the odds will be on your side.

13

BE PASSIONATE—IT'S THE ONLY WAY TO MOVE MOUNTAINS

Building Trump International Golf Club

When I decided to build my first golf course, I found a good piece of land near my Mar-a-Lago estate in Palm Beach and decided to go all out. I hired Jim Fazio, one of the all-time great golf course designers. When he told me he'd have to move over three million cubic yards of dirt to make the relatively flat land into a spectacular course, I didn't blink an eye. I was excited about building my first golf course and ready to move mountains if necessary.

I did, however, wonder what I'd gotten myself into once again. Shortly after hearing the three million number, he told

Palm Beach

me it would be necessary to bring in over five thousand trees, and about a thousand royal palms, and over a thousand coconut trees. Then there would need to be about $2 million worth of little plants to make everything look well groomed. The water feature for one hole, number 17, would cost close to $3 million dollars and take about nine months to complete. This was going to be an 18-hole course. I almost started to worry.

I knew Jim was giving me straight, well-thought out numbers for his work. His integrity is legend. This is simply how much it costs to get an extraordinary piece of work done, I told myself.

THE LOW POINT

I realized that my original $40 million estimate might be way too low. Is this what happens when a developer who specializes in skyscrapers turns to golf course development? Was I making a huge mistake? Should I have stuck with terrain that I knew more about already?

I've always told people to know what they were doing first, to do due diligence to the nth degree, to be cautiously optimistic. I suddenly found myself wondering why I didn't heed my own advice. I was facing a lot of new issues where I wasn't yet an expert. However, I was excited about the fact that we were building something outstanding, and that kept me going.

Jim Fazio often says that one of the great things about working with me is that I never asked him if we were spending too much money. Instead I'd ask, "Do you need anything else?" He said that attitude helped his creative process. I'm glad he thought that because in a big way that's how it was. I have to admit that I had a few moments of doubts. Not big doubts, but doubts nevertheless.

For example, it took a solid year to move three million cubic yards of dirt and to transplant five thousand trees. This wasn't fast going, but it was necessary, and it was painstaking work on Jim's part. Then, the Department of Environmental Resources told us that only 50 acres could be cleared at a time, which required us to plan the course in seven sections. This also involved labeling all the trees and building a lake system. So it took a year before the golf course could even begin to be built.

Fortunately, I'm a patient man when it comes to things I care a lot about. I was very excited to have a spectacular course, and I realized that if this is what was required to have that, then so be it. I had made my decision, and I decided to stick with it. I also knew I had a real pro working for me. Jim Fazio's reputation preceded him, and I could see for myself that he was totally reliable as well as genuinely passionate about his work. Was I expecting the impossible?

When you are faced with situations like these, it's important to think about why you are doing whatever you're doing in the first place. There are always going to be some problems, and if you can remind yourself of your original goal, it helps to clarify and shed light on any doubts you might be having. Having done that, I was reassured and ready to move forward.

Then I heard about the oak trees. One thousand of them. It took five months to move them in because each of them had to be wrapped and only three could be hauled in at a time. These oak trees were 20 to 40 feet tall each. They would line the fairways and would be worth it. I hoped.

It was around this time I heard about the gopher tortoises. This was definitely a new dilemma. I'm used to zoning problems, but tortoises? Sixty of them in fact. They had to be cared for, absolutely. We were entering their turf, and we wanted to make sure we found an equal or better environment for them. Safely relocating them became a priority. I learned a lot about gopher tortoises. For example, they have been known to dig burrows as long as 40 feet by 10 feet deep. Just imagine what that could do to a golf course! So while I admired the tortoises for their industry, they had to be carefully relocated.

After more than a year of meticulous preparation, the course was actually being built. Every hole was treated as if it was to be the culmination of a great course, and the end result is that the course is an absolute masterpiece. No other description does it justice.

That's what I wanted, and that's what I got. Every tree was worth the time and effort (and believe me, I know about each and every tree). An additional nine hole course was opened in 2006 to equal acclaim. It was been a resounding success on top of being an extraordinary achievement of design.

The success and beauty of Trump International Golf Club set me up for building more golf courses, and all of them have been highly praised and very successful. Each course came with its own set of challenges, but after tackling my first course, I was ready for them. Moving mountains? Moving tortoises? No problem.

COACH TRUMP
MAKE IT HAPPEN IN YOUR LIFE

My point to you is this: If you are passionate about your endeavors, it will be reflected back to you in your end result. Be sure to get the right people to work with you—Jim Fazio is as passionate about his work as I am and this becomes apparent when you see the scope and quality of the finished course. Overcoming tremendous obstacles is all in a day's work—if you love what you're doing. Remember that.

14

IF YOU SEE BIG
PROBLEMS, LOOK FOR
BIG OPPORTUNITIES

*Transforming a Dilapidated
Neighborhood into a
World-Class Hot Spot*

Today, Grand Central Station in New York City is beautiful, both as a sight as well as a site. It's in a thriving, well-kept neighborhood. However, in the 1970s, it was a different situation altogether. The area was in the midst of serious decay. It was crummy, run down, and a destination point for no one except those entering and leaving the city as quickly as they possibly could. Who could blame them? If this depressing area truly represented New York City, I'd want to leave, too.

I'm a New Yorker. I love this city, always have and always will. So this situation merited my attention, and the opportunity, as I saw it, was not just to turn an old hotel into a shiny new one, but to bring up the neighborhood at the same time. It's that "think big" attitude that I have. Why do one thing when you can accomplish two or more at the same time?

The old Commodore Hotel next to Grand Central was in big trouble. It was a disgraceful sight. The people passing by were on their way to good jobs, coming from good homes and they would continue this daily trek unless the city folded up and went goodbye, which wasn't likely to happen. I knew that the neighborhood was ready for change, and acquiring the Commodore Hotel became a quest.

Even my father couldn't believe I was serious. He said "buying the Commodore at a time when even the Chrysler Building is in bankruptcy is like fighting for a seat on the Titanic." He knew it was a risk and so did I. The flip side was that I knew it was a way to get the city to flourish the way it should. I'd be creating jobs and improving the neighborhood, for starters. I wanted it to be beautiful, and that gave me incentive to get through all the problems and negativity surrounding this project. That's a good thing to keep in mind—use your mind to visualize how things might be, as you go along. That can make the plethora of details and setbacks just a part of the plan.

About nine months before I was seriously into negotiations for the hotel, the owner—Penn Central Railroad—spent about $2 million in renovations that had no impact whatsoever. The hotel needed far more work. Six million dollars was owed in back taxes. It was not a pleasant situation for the owners, and they were ready to get out. Before I could purchase the hotel for $10 million, I had to structure an extremely complex deal with other interested parties. I needed a tax abatement from the City of New York, commitment from a hotel company with experience running hotels, and financing. This was complicated stuff and it took several years to negotiate everything.

At one point, Penn Central wanted me to pay a nonrefundable $250,000 for an exclusive option on the property. I had to stall on that. That was a lot of money for an obviously risky situation. In order to remain in the process but to have more time, I had my lawyers nitpick the contracts and slow everything down.

Meanwhile, I looked for a designer who had what it took to make a spectacular building. One young architect named Der Scutt that I contacted was immediately interested. He understood that I wanted to change the dingy hotel completely, to basically wrap it in something new and shiny and give the whole area a new face.

Note that I wasn't sure this deal was even going to go through, but because my goal was so clear in my mind, I went ahead and took the time to meet with an architect, as if the project was a done deal. That's positive thinking, but also pragmatic thinking—keep things moving forward! If one thing doesn't work out, another will. Meantime, I will have met and connected with an architect that I respected and who respected me. If this deal fell through, I'd already know someone to reach out to for the next big project.

I hired Der Scutt to do some drawings and asked him to make the presentation look as sleek as possible. I also started to look for an operator for the hotel. The hotel business was new to me at the time, so I needed to find someone with experience, a lot of it, because my proposal was for a 1,400-room hotel with 1.5 million square feet. That's big.

I wanted a big operator, and the big names then were Hilton, Hyatt, Sheraton, Holiday Inn, and Ramada Inn. To me, the top of the line was Hyatt. Their hotels were contemporary and light, which would be the perfect antidote to the dark and dreary Commodore. It was also a fact that they didn't have a presence in New York City, though Hilton did. They might be interested.

I was correct—they were. I called up the president, and we discussed a partnership. However, he was prone to changing his mind after we'd negotiate, and this was seriously interfering with any progress. So I called another executive at Hyatt who suggested I call the guy who really ran the company, Jay Pritzker of the Pritzker family, who owned a controlling interest in Hyatt, so I did. He seemed eager to meet me and came to New York. We made a deal quickly, as equal partners. Hyatt would manage the hotel after I had it built. I was thrilled. We announced it to the press in May of 1975.

I still needed to get financing—and a multimillion dollar tax abatement from the city. At least with a hotel partner, an architect, and rough cost estimates, I had something substantial to bring with me along with my big ideas. So I hired a real estate broker who had a lot of experience, and who was in his sixties. I was only 27 years old at this time, and having a mature, accomplished presence with me worked to my advantage. We'd be making the pitch together for financing and we'd make a good pair. That's a good point to remember—get the right people to work with you. When dealing with Hyatt, it was critical that I had gone around the president who was slowing things down and called Jay Pritzker directly. Now, finding a dedicated broker who added the right balance to my image was a smart move. Am I tooting my own horn a bit? You bet.

Getting financing quickly became a catch-22 situation: Without financing, the city wasn't about to consider a tax abatement, and without a tax abatement, the banks weren't too keen on financing. It seemed like a brick wall at every turn, so we decided to change our approach. We appealed to the bankers' guilt about the decaying city and the fact that they were choosing to look the other way when someone (like me) had a great idea to change things for the better. I'd be changing a prime area that was headed toward becoming a slum into a vibrant new place. How could they not want to be involved? Of course, that didn't work.

THE LOW POINT

Here was the moment of truth. We finally found a bank that appeared to be interested. We went far with them, putting in endless hours and effort, when a key guy suddenly changed his mind and brought up some inconsequential issue in order to kill the deal. We came up with every conceivable argument, but the guy was implacable. He would not budge. It was at this point that I said to my broker, "Let's just take this deal and shove it." I had had it.

You're probably surprised to even hear me say it, but it's one of the few times I just wanted to throw in the towel. It was my broker and my lawyer, George Ross, who convinced me to keep going, pointing out how much time and effort had already been devoted to this project. I quickly resolved to stick it out and see this through. I'm not a quitter by nature, but I'm telling you this so you'll know there have been times when the difficulties seemed greater than the rewards. That was definitely the low point, but because I hung in there, it became a turning point. Afterward my resolution became even *stronger*.

I decided to approach the city, even without financing, and explain the situation: the Hyatt hotel organization was anxious to come to New York, but the costs were too high—unless the city gave us a break on property taxes. I was blunt and to the point, and it was effective. The city agreed to a deal that would essentially make us partners, and I would receive a property tax abatement for 40 years. It was a deal that benefited everyone. I would buy the Commodore for $10 million, with $6 million going to the city for back taxes. I would then sell the hotel to the city for one dollar, and they would lease it back to me for 99 years.

Was this complicated? Yes, but it worked, and we eventually got financing from two institutions. One of them was directly across the street from the Commodore. I don't think they wanted their neighborhood to continue into decline, which they knew it was headed for. They knew a new and beautiful hotel could bring their area back to prime time, prime space, and prime business.

THE RESULT

I don't know if you have seen the Hyatt at Grand Central, but it has four exterior walls of mirrors as a façade—which reflect all the wonderful architecture of the area. Incredibly, this at first made people furious because it didn't fit in with the existing neighborhood design. What they didn't realize is that the reflections of the surrounding buildings emphasized their beauty and importance to the Manhattan skyline. Now, people and critics love this building. It started the revitalization of the Grand Central area and opened in 1980 to great success. Today, it's a hub of New York City—thriving and beautiful. I'm very happy for my sake and for the city of New York that I didn't decide to give up on this one.

COACH TRUMP
MAKE IT HAPPEN IN YOUR LIFE

Expect problems and setbacks. It's all part of the game. If you're not running into major challenges, you're doing something easy, and probably not that valuable—and it's probably not going to make much money for you. A big problem often signals a big opportunity. Be prepared to work long and hard for it.

Don't be afraid to pursue multiple options, or multiple people, at the same time. If one thing doesn't work out, you've got back-up options. I promise you, not everything is going to work. In fact, you may have to try a lot of things to get just one thing to work. That's tenacity, and it's critical to success.

15

CULTIVATE A SENSE
OF DISCOVERY

A Letter from My
Kindergarten Teacher

I receive a lot of mail every day—piles of it. Not too long ago I received a letter from my kindergarten teacher. It was a big surprise for me to come across that in one of those piles of letters. She mentioned that what she remembered most clearly about me is that I never stopped asking questions. I was the most inquisitive student she had ever had. I wrote back to her that some things never change—I still ask a lot of questions—but that my curiosity and sense of discovery has served me well for all these years. I also thanked her, belatedly, for her patience many years ago, listening to all my questions.

I started thinking back to those early days. Every one of my questions was the beginning of a new discovery back then, and that's how it is with me today. I hope it's the same with you. Maybe your own sense of discovery is one reason you're reading this book.

Emerson's quote, "What lies behind us, and what lies before us, are tiny matters compared to what lies within us" is a good thought to keep in mind. It allows your mind to think big because there are big reservoirs of ideas inside all of us. It's a way to open the channels of creative thought, which leads to discovery and achievement. It's also a reminder that no matter how much you've accomplished already, there's still more waiting for you to get done.

Maybe I'm a naturally curious person, but I think it's a good attitude to cultivate. I like hearing what other people have to say, and I learn a lot that way, too. My interests are reflected in the diversity of businesses that I am involved in—real estate, the entertainment industry, golf course development, and so forth. Keeping yourself as diverse as possible can open you up to many more opportunities than you might imagine. Sometimes one thing can lead to another.

You already know I'm not big on complacency, and I'm also not big on know-it-alls. The more you know, the more you realize how much you don't know. Having this attitude is a great way to set yourself up for some big success. To be any other way is to sell yourself short. How can you possibly discover anything if you already know everything?

People who come into my office for the first time are often surprised by how many questions I ask. I remember when I had three bathroom sinks on a couch just outside my office for a few weeks. I had to decide which one I liked the best, so I asked every person who came in for their opinion and the reasons behind their choice. You'd be amazed at how much that opened up conversation and discussion, and I learned some very insightful things about these people and their tastes.

Give yourself a chance—cultivate a sense of discovery.

16

KNOW WHEN TO CUT YOUR LOSSES

TRUMP SHUTTLE

How do you decide when it is smarter to bail out than to keep paddling?

As businesses go, I'd rate the airlines as a great idea if you want a lot of trouble, too much competition, too much work, and all for too little profit. Recently, we saw what happened to JetBlue. They'd had a great record, very pleased passengers, and one ice storm knocked their reputation and their credibility completely off the runway. Their popularity plummeted and they had to issue a public apology to passengers for their mismanagement. I thought, "that's the airline business for you." Even Delta Airlines, which has been established for a long time, is just recently coming out of bankruptcy.

TRUMP: NEVER GIVE UP

The reason I can wince knowingly about these episodes with airlines is that I owned one, from 1989 to 1992. It was known as the Trump Shuttle, and it was originally a part of Eastern Air Lines. We had flights from LaGuardia Airport in New York City to Boston and Washington, DC, on an hourly basis. I got into the business initially because Eastern Airlines was having trouble in the late 1980s and it began selling its routes, including its northeastern air shuttle. This route was heavily traveled and I knew it could be successful. It just needed to be buffed up a bit, to make the travel time a bit more luxurious for the passengers.

My previous experience with air travel was that I owned a helicopter service that provided flights to Atlantic City, La Guardia, Manhattan, the Hamptons, and Hartford and I also had a private jet. I knew the conveniences that a traveler would want to have. I made the new shuttle top of the line and technologically savvy, with one of the first self-service check-in kiosks, and it had laptop computers available to rent. The 727s were completely redecorated with maple wood trim inside and beautiful fixtures. I was the first to provide real luxury for shuttle passengers, who had been used to no-frills transportation.

THE LOW POINT

We hit a perfect storm. I went into this business knowing that Eastern Airlines was in trouble, and in fact I acquired the shuttle during a threatened mechanics strike. Let's just say there were problems, but I'm used to problems, right? Well, airline problems are another story entirely. The labor strike happened, and it went on long enough that we lost a lot of passengers to

Amtrak as well as to the Pan Am Shuttle. In addition, we were entering into a recession, and then in 1990, jet fuel prices sky-rocketed due to the Iraqi invasion of Kuwait. If it wasn't one thing, it was another. It's such a delicate business that the slightest tremor in world politics, economics, labor, or the weather—and a hundred other variables—can make a bright future suddenly tumble.

As you know, I was having some financial problems around this time that would begin to escalate, not diminish, due to the recession that had hit. My total demise was predicted in 1991 by the *Wall Street Journal* and the *New York Times*. I had several big things falter, but this wasn't 1991 yet, it was 1990. I was sure Trump Shuttle would take off and avoid the recession. I was wrong. Trump Shuttle never turned a proper profit, and as my other business interests started to fail, my creditors were less than enthusiastic about my latest venture. In September of 1990, the ownership of the airline went to Citicorp, the airline's creditor bank. It's a complicated story, but to make it short, Trump Shuttle finally ended as such in April of 1992, and it was merged into a new corporation, which US Airways bought.

I have to admit I was relieved to be out of that business. The timing wasn't right, but as I've watched the airline industry, I wonder if the timing is *ever* right. Making a profit isn't easy, and it's a demanding and volatile business. That's why I find it hard to believe that Richard Branson, the owner of Virgin Air, has made any money at all with his airline. Fortunately he has other businesses, or I don't think he'd be where he is today financially.

In the instance of Trump Shuttle, I know I did what was right to make it a successful and desirable business. I made the experience better for the traveler and introduced some innovations. It didn't matter—the outside forces were too great. It's one of those instances when you know the best decision is the decision to leave, to cut your losses and move on to something else. It was a great learning experience—of what business *not* to go into. I'm perfectly happy now with my own planes. I rarely fly on commercial airlines and I can't say I miss it. I certainly don't miss the business.

COACH TRUMP
MAKE IT HAPPEN IN YOUR LIFE

Sometimes you work as hard as you can on something, and it doesn't work out. The question is: How do you know when to give up? I usually tough it out longer than most people would in a similar situation—which is why I often succeed where others have failed. I also know that sometimes you have to throw in the towel. Maybe you failed, but you probably learned something valuable. Chalk it up to experience, don't take it personally, and go find your next challenge!

17

BUSINESS IS ABOUT
KNOWING THE WORLD

There are probably a million definitions of what business is, what it isn't, what it's about, how it works, and so forth. Years ago, I realized an important thing: Business is about knowing the world. That's a big assignment. That realization opened me up to a myriad of great opportunities I hadn't seen before.

I started to see the world as an emerging market. That insight alone can improve your vision almost automatically (and vision is necessary for great success). In fact, if you can begin to see your neighborhood, your town, your state, as an emerging market, you will be surprised at how creative you will become. New ideas will come to you even though you know every street, every house, every tree. Newness of vision can be invaluable when it comes to business.

When you suddenly get some great idea, ask yourself, "What am I pretending not to see?" That's a good test for blind spots. Don't throw out those sudden lightning-like ideas, but be circumspect about them.

Knowing the world means seeing the whole picture. That is definitely preferable to seeing a narrow slice of life and being content with a small amount of local knowledge. What we don't know can be as important as what we do know. If that thought doesn't make you endlessly curious about the wide world, I don't know what will. It's imperative to keep the big picture in mind and stay hungry for learning more, if you want big success.

I have had a "think big" attitude for a long time, even when I was determined to succeed in Manhattan as a young man. That was an immediate goal. The ultimate goal was a bit more universal. However, you have to do first things first. Now I am developing in many countries throughout the world, and the Trump brand is known globally. That's no accident.

Aside from great determination and a strong will, I have to say that understanding the realities of how the world works, including a sense of world history, is a necessary ingredient for wide-ranging success. There may be flukes that will occur that catapult individuals to fame or fortune, but most often you will find that people who have operated on a large scale and remained diligent and successful for a long time also have a broad understanding of world.

I think the way technology drives business around the world today is an example of this. Visionaries saw all of this happening before most of us had given it a thought. The Internet has brought the world together in an exciting and efficient way, and all of us, worldwide, are affected. Technology is growing so rapidly that it's hard to keep up with the changes, even if you're in the industry. People have said, "but is all this change really necessary?" My answer is that refrigerators aren't really necessary, the world functioned without them for many centuries, but they sure were a great invention. In fact, for many years, countries' reputations were in part based on whether they had refrigeration or not.

Emerging markets is a term very often associated with Wall Street firms. They have entire departments dedicated to fast-growing markets in developing countries around the world. Places like China, Brazil, Russia, Korea, and so on are making a big impact on the world economy. If you live in this world, it's a good thing to know something about it because it will most likely affect you and your business goals.

My advice is to change your compass from local to global—while minding your local business. It may take an extra hour a day, but I can assure you it will be well worth your time and effort. How do I know this? What country do you live in? Have you ever heard of Trump? There's your answer.

18

If You Think You Can Complete a Six-Year Project in Six Months, You Probably Can

*Wollman Rink, Central Park,
New York City*

Very often, what I want to do involves a lot of other organizations and a lot of bureaucracy. They say you can't fight city hall, but I have no problem going against conventional wisdom. Think for yourself and go ahead and fight, especially if it means enough to you. This particular fight had a personal element to it—the view out my living room window.

My apartment in Trump Tower overlooks the historic and scenic Wollman Rink in Central Park. It's a beautiful winter

Wollman Rink

scene to look out and see it filled with ice skaters—except that for six years it was closed, and to look at the empty rink for six winters in a row finally got to me. This is a story about doing something that wasn't going to be easy, in fact it was deliberately walking into a mess, but the end result would be a happy story for a lot of citizens in New York City as well as thousands of visitors. It was a labor of love that also turned out to be one of my favorite accomplishments.

New York City's management fiasco with the renovation of Wollman Rink was an absolute classic. After six years of renovations to the tune of $12 million, the rink was still closed. Then the city announced in 1986 that the entire process of renovation was starting over again, from scratch. I could bear it no more and wrote to then Mayor Koch offering to construct a brand-new Wollman Rink and have it done in six months, at no cost to the city. It would be my gift to this great city.

This sincere gesture was spurned by Mayor Koch, but he published my letter in New York papers as a joke. Unfortunately for him, the New York journalists and public rallied to my side. He totally underestimated the press reaction. As one paper wrote, "The city has proved nothing except that it can't get the job done." Koch's reaction to my magnanimous gesture reminded me of the old saying, "No good deed goes unpunished."

The next day, after the papers and public took my side, Koch reversed himself completely. Suddenly, the city was virtually begging me to take on Wollman Rink. We had a meeting in my office on June 6, 1986, with city officials, and long story short, we came to an agreement. I put up the construction money and agreed to complete the work by December 15. At that point, the city would reimburse me for my costs, up to a cap of just less than $3 million, but only if the rink worked. If I came in under budget, the city would pay me back only what I'd spent. If I went over budget, I'd cover the overruns myself.

THE LOW POINT

Although I was genuinely interested in doing this renovation, I must admit that when I went over and saw the conditions I was walking into, I had a few moments of doubt. This rink is over an acre in size, which makes it one of the largest man-made rinks in the country. There were enormous holes in the roof of the skaters' house, there had been extensive water damage, and the rink required 22 miles of pipes. It also required two 35,000-pound refrigeration units. I had publicly promised to complete all the work within six months! I wondered if I had backed myself into a potentially humiliating corner. If I failed, it would be in all the papers, and my reputation would definitely suffer. I had some challenges ahead of me, that's for sure. The doubts went away as long as I kept the image of a beautiful and finished rink in my mind. I knew I could get it done, but I wasn't kidding myself that it would be a piece of cake.

The physical conditions at the rink weren't the biggest problem. There was such a lack of direction that the restoration process looked like a bumper car amusement ride that just went round and round in circles. There was no leadership. That's when I made the decision to take charge and check on this project every single day. I wanted to know what was going on, who was doing what, and I personally oversaw the progress. For example, because I knew nothing about building rinks, I set out to find the best skating-rink builder I could. I spoke to experts and decided on a brine system for refrigerating the ice. It's more costly but very durable. I approached every aspect of rebuilding the rink as a personal undertaking.

The rink was finished one month ahead of time—and under budget. It was well worth the effort. The gala opening celebration for the rink was a great occasion, and we had skaters Peggy Fleming, Dorothy Hamill, Scott Hamilton, and others to help celebrate this great day for New York City. We finally had a working rink and a beautiful place for New Yorkers to play. All profits went to charity and the Parks Department. Everyone won.

Was this process easy? No, it was painstaking. Was it worth it? You better believe it. When you come to New York City, don't miss it. Skating under the trees in Central Park and looking out on the magnificent skyline is an event you will never forget.

POSTSCRIPT TO THE WOLLMAN
RINK STORY—21 YEARS LATER

Government bungling of the Wollman Rink project was made possible in part thanks to a terrible New York State law passed in 1921 called the Wicks Law. It requires local governments undertaking renovations or new building projects that cost more $50,000 to hire four separate contractors (general construction, plumbing, electrical, and heating and ventilation). Local governments must hire the lowest bidder in each of these areas, even though they could save a lot of time and money by hiring a single general contractor who oversees all subcontractors. Instead of allowing competition, what it does is increase up to 30 percent the cost of building anything for the government in New York.

Fortunately, there may be some new hope for getting rid of the Wicks Law thanks to recent media attention. On May 29, 2007, the *New York Times* ran an article by Dorothy Samuels in their Editorial section which was titled *From Donald Trump to Eliot Spitzer: Still Battling Over a Wasteful Law*. Ms. Samuels has always been an insightful writer who writes about significant issues. In bringing up the Wicks Law, she retold the story of how I saved Wollman Rink from government bungling—and managed to educate the citizens of New York City about something they probably weren't aware of, unless they are in real estate construction. It's something that affects them by driving up government costs and taxes. I have to say, it was nice to be remembered 21 years later as someone who tried to make a difference, and did. Let's hope this situation will be remedied soon—it will benefit everyone.

19

DON'T LET FEAR STOP YOU—EVEN IN FRONT OF MILLIONS OF PEOPLE

Doubts Will Continue to Surface, Even after You've Made Up Your Mind to Go Forward

A *SATURDAY NIGHT LIVE* STORY

What do you do when doubts continue to surface, even after you've committed to go forward? A lot of people mistakenly think that I stride the planet in a state of absolute certainty, all of the time. The truth is, there are times I have to wrestle with doubts after I've made big decisions. The challenge is what you do with doubts. Handled poorly, doubt can sap your spirit and resolve. Handled well, doubt should make you smarter and strengthen your chances for success.

I will always remember the day Jeff Zucker, the president of NBC, called to make an appointment to see me in my office. *The Apprentice* was already the hit of the season on NBC, and I didn't think he'd be making a social call, considering the schedules both of us keep. However, I was not prepared when he came in and said to me, "Donald, do me a favor. Host *Saturday Night Live*."

Hosting *Saturday Night Live* is usually a job reserved for professional entertainers, from Billy Crystal to Kevin Spacey, from Robin Williams to Alec Baldwin. While I was honored to be asked, I wondered if this was a very big chance to make a fool of myself. I had a few moments of doubts like that and then realized it would be a great opportunity as well as a great challenge. It might even be fun. I said yes.

THE LOW POINT

I didn't really know what I was getting myself into, but it was too late now. After Jeff left, I started thinking of a live audience, comedy skits, a monologue, facing off with Darrell Hammond, who imitates me very well, and who knows what else they'd come up with. This is a particularly good story for this book because it illustrates how doubts—potentially one of the worst forms of adversity—can continue to surface, even after you've made up your mind to go forward—courageously—with some big risk. Let me tell you, I had major doubts about this one. It's not always smooth sailing just because you've decided to do something with enthusiasm. Running through my mind was the fact that if the show was a disaster, millions of people would witness it, live, without edits. It was great opportunity to flop on a huge level. The doubts swelled, and I knew I had to regroup.

The more I thought about it, I realized: the show is legendary, I knew its creator, Lorne Michaels, and the writers are fantastic. I knew I'd give it my best shot. As I've always said, you've got to think big.

Anyway, the process of this live show was an incredible experience. First, on Tuesday, I met with Lorne's team of gifted writers, led by Tina Fey. They asked questions and pitched a lot of ideas. It was an intense and productive hour. By Thursday, we were reading through the sketches with the members of the *Saturday Night Live* team. They are pros but very amiable and helpful, so it was a pleasure and I felt some of my nervousness vanishing. I knew I was facing some pretty big hurdles, and I was wondering how it would all fall into place in the two days we had. I was also wondering how I would remember everything. I'm used to doing my own material, and as a public speaker, I'm at ease. However, this was a different scenario entirely.

Our first full day was on Friday, where we did run-throughs of the skits on the *Saturday Night Live* stage. The sets weren't finished, but the theatrical aspect of what I was getting into was very apparent. There was so much going on around me that I didn't have time to take into account the fact that I was feeling apprehensive—they had me in a lot of skits. I would be a hippie in a business meeting, the author of a romance novel, a lawyer, a character in *The Prince and the Pauper* along with Darrell Hammond, a keyboard player, and more. In addition, the costume changes had to be taken into consideration. There wasn't much time between skits, and one skit required a mid-skit costume change. Fortunately, they have a wardrobe team that later takes over and navigates you through the show. Since I'm a guy who likes to know everything that's going on, I will admit that a few times I felt a bit overwhelmed.

Things were going pretty well, and my confidence level was improving, especially when I saw that the *Saturday Night Live* regulars were enjoying the proceedings and having a few good laughs themselves. Then, I saw my costume for the chicken wings number. This was a commercial for Trump's House of Wings, a skit that was popular from the first time we tried it out. It involves singing chickens, with me in the middle of them. I don't need to say more. I had already said the chicken outfit was out, and what they gave me instead wasn't much better: a bright yellow polyester suit that would make anyone look like a sitting duck for smart comments. I remember saying to someone, "What have I gotten myself into?"

Little did I know the hard part was coming: the monologue. Think about it: walking out on stage with millions of people watching, and hoping to be funny. Then think about this: What if I wasn't funny? Here's a word to the wise—don't think about it! You have to go for it or you will just freeze up thinking about it.

I want to stop here to reiterate what I just wrote. It is absolutely true that sometimes you just have to get out there and do it. Being tentative can lend itself to fear, and fear of failure can halt you immediately. You have to work despite your fears, and very often they will disappear. Don't let fear stop you!

I know, it's easier said than done. I even said to the set builders at this point, "What am I doing here? I should be building, like you. I can relate to you guys." Once I got deeper into the rehearsals, it went well. We got some good laughs, which, believe me, was a wonderful sound, and I had gotten through a very big test of my ability to handle pressure and a new environment. In fact, I remember thinking that maybe I'd ask Darrell over to my office one day, so I could take a break and he could play me for a few hours. Thinking these thoughts managed to take my mind off the live show the next night. It was all still very new to me.

The next day was Saturday, which ends up being a marathon day for everyone. We ran through the show for a live audience of three hundred people. This was considered to be the dress rehearsal, and the skits that are most popular with this audience will make the final show. That's when I learned that we wouldn't know what skits would be in the live show, or their order, until about a half hour before appearing live. I'm someone who likes having things in order and ready to go, no matter what it might be, this news hit me with a strange sense of surprise. I'm used to having and studying blueprints for a long time, for example. Being well prepared for critical meetings has been one of the secrets to my success. Just think, some of the skits we had rehearsed for two days would be cut out completely, including, it turned out, one of my favorites where I played a romance novelist. All the preparations for those skits would be null and void. Then we'd have a new running order and no time to get ready for it. I was in for an exciting time, that's for sure.

I had to take a deep breath and realize that I just might be in over my head. This was big time, with a huge live audience to watch me as well as being on tape for history to see. My photo would go up on the wall in the halls of the legendary show. What if I flopped? Forgot my lines? Forgot the lyrics to the song I had to learn in five minutes? Put on the wrong costume? Looked like an idiot instead of a respected real estate developer? Believe me, you can have a lot of thoughts at critical moments like these. So if you've ever felt that way, know you're in some good company. Here's my advice—get to it and go on with the show!

That's what I did, and beginning with the monologue, I have to say it was a night I'll always remember. Everyone had a good time, from the wardrobe people to the *Saturday Night Live* pros, to the audiences, both live and at home, and to the musicians who made sure we were ready to go on when the time came. Here's the best part—I had a fantastic time, and an experience that was worth every nagging thought and fear of failure thought that crossed my mind during that hectic week. Did I ever think I'd be the host of *Saturday Night Live*? Never! That's what's great about taking chances. Success won't happen to you unless you decide to take chances first. Don't settle for failure when you can take a few risks and change the course of your life, or at least enhance it. It may not be *Saturday Night Live*, but taking risks and putting yourself in uncomfortable new situations can definitely put some excitement into your life. If I can do a song and dance number with people dressed up like chickens, in a bright yellow suit, in front of millions of people, you can certainly stand to take a chance once in a while. I don't want to hear any excuses. So go for it and never give up!

COACH TRUMP
MAKE IT HAPPEN IN YOUR LIFE

Be a chameleon. When a challenging opportunity comes along, take full advantage of it. Learn from it. Taking risks and making mistakes is the best way to learn something new. Most of the time, you will surprise yourself.

Just dive in. Don't give yourself time to doubt. If you're thinking, "I'm not sure if I can do this," turn it into, "It's going to feel great when I do this!"

20

DON'T TAKE YOURSELF
TOO SERIOUSLY

P eople are surprised sometimes when they visit our offices
and hear laughter coming from mine. I'm a serious businessman but I also know the value of laughter. That's why I
smile when I see those long serious faces in ads and commercials
that are supposed to represent serious business being done.
There's no reason you can't have some fun. In fact, if you're not
having fun, you know by now that I would advise you to find
something else to do. Your job is probably not brain surgery, so
lighten up a little.

A friend of mine, Joel Anderson, is a remarkable and very
successful businessman. I had invited him to a major charity
event, and I didn't hear back from him until after the event had
happened. He had been traveling, but he took the time to write
me a note and send a check anyway. He explained that thanks to
The Apprentice, I had become so famous that he was able to sell

the signature on my letter for enough money to cover the charitable donation he was enclosing. I wrote back thanking him and told him I like having shrewd friends who know a good business deal when they see one. Both of us had a good laugh, and a good cause benefited.

That's one way business works, and it can make every day a pleasure. Try to spice up your dealings and daily work routine with occasional jokes and laughter, and you'll see how much more enjoyable your work will become. The people you work with will appreciate it, too, if you can make them laugh.

After the first season of *The Apprentice*, I wrote Mark Burnett a letter about how it had been a fantastic experience working with him. I explained to him that little did I know while writing *The Art of the Deal* back in 1987 that it would become a bestseller while at the same time being a catalyst to a young man selling T-shirts on Venice Beach in California. (That young man was Mark Burnett.) I also told him that if I'd ever said anything negative about guys who hang out on the beach, that "I hereby take it back." We had become business partners but also friends, and the humor we enjoyed made the experience all the better.

It pays to have a sense of humor about yourself. I did a commercial for VISA a few years ago that required me to grovel around (or appear to be groveling around) in a dumpster to retrieve my VISA card. I was filmed on top of Trump Tower showing my card, when a gust of wind blows it out of my hand and onto the street below. A passerby notes when I crawl out of the dumpster, "And I thought he was doing so well!" I didn't mind—I had a great time and the commercial was a big success. If I took myself too seriously, I would have missed out on a lot of fun and a nice paycheck. Business at its best should have both.

21

Sometimes You Have
to Start Over

Dubai

Sometimes it's in your best interest to start over, even if
you're established and can afford to do as you please. A good
example of that is the new Palm Trump International Hotel &
Tower that's going up in Dubai. I think most of us have heard of
Dubai by now, in the United Arab Emirates. Just off the coast is
a man-made palm-tree-shaped island, the Palm Jumeirah, that is
a remarkable achievement of engineering and imagination. I
partnered with Nakheel, the developer of over $30 billion in
real estate in Dubai, to build a tower on this island.

Nakheel, in Arabic, means *palm trees*, so it follows that this
would be their imprint in the Arabian Gulf. In 2005, we went
into partnership and agreed that our hotel, which will be the

luxury pivot point of the Palm Jumeirah, should be an extraordinary example of design and innovation. We both had the experience, the credentials, and the desire to do something amazing.

One thing that attracted me to Nakheel, aside from their proven record of success and expertise, was their innovative approach to whatever they did. Our original design for the hotel garnered a lot of publicity. It was a tulip design that would have a state-of-the-art exoskeleton frame. We were excited about this iconic design. The price tag would be $400 million to complete it.

However, after reviewing the design, we realized there were some problems with it, and we agreed it looked a bit heavy. So we decided to start over. We just scrapped it. Don't ever be afraid to change your mind about something. There is nothing wrong with that. Yes, we'd spent time and money on the first design, but when you're going after the extraordinary, sometimes you have to take extraordinary pains to achieve it.

The new design we came up with was stunning: a split tower, with an open core design. It would cost $600 million for 48 stories and would be constructed with glass, stainless steel, and stone. It would definitely be worth it. We expect the tower to be finished in 2009.

There are considerations beyond the usual when you are developing internationally, and sure enough, in February 2006, we were hit with a political/global trade controversy involving Dubai that threatened the viability of the project. Major world events can crop up at any time, and sometimes I feel like saying, now what? However, that's part of the deal. It can be a challenge—but it's always enlightening.

Anyway, the controversy was over the sale of shipping port management businesses in six major U.S. seaports to a company that was based in the United Arab Emirates. This received huge attention as a national security debate in the United States. The

Dubai Sunrise

question was whether such a sale would compromise port security. This put Dubai in the national and international spotlight. For us, that could be good and that could be bad. The good news was that suddenly everyone knew where Dubai was. The bad news is that controversy, especially concerning national security, could work against spreading the message about Dubai being a fantastic destination. It took us time to fully comprehend the echo effect of this controversy.

I found it interesting that this development followed shortly after our deal went through in the United Arab Emirates, but all we could do was ride it out. I was relieved when it was resolved quickly and amicably. Eventually, U.S. security concerns were addressed, and Dubai demonstrated it understood the importance of security.

We are looking forward to a 2010 opening in Dubai, and I already know it's been worth every change and every challenge. There may be a few more challenges along the way but I'll be ready for them.

COACH TRUMP
MAKE IT HAPPEN IN YOUR LIFE

Be resilient. Sometimes a challenge will knock you down. Your plan may be a bust or your goal may be unattainable for a time; you may be stopped in your tracks. Get back on the horse! Deciding to try again is the first step toward getting it right the next time.

22

I TOLD MY FRIEND HE
WAS A BIG TIME LOSER

The Power of Focus

I'm fortunate to have the capacity to change my thought patterns quickly—to focus on something new without a long adjustment period. For example, people have commented on how quickly I conduct meetings; I can lead effective and productive meetings one after another without any downtime between them. I credit this ability to knowing what focus really is and the ability to get to the point very quickly.

My focus is always on the solution to whatever the problem—or challenge—might be. In contrast, I have met so many people who waste a lot of their time (and mine) talking about their problems. It becomes very clear to me that they are avoiding looking for a solution. They either like the drama of their situation or are too lazy to make the effort of using their brains to look at solutions.

Thinking takes energy and it shouldn't be wasted dwelling on the wrong things. For every problem there is a solution, and capable people will look for that solution. Make sure you're one of the capable people.

Getting to the point is sometimes just a matter of asking yourself the right questions and answering them honestly. I remember an old friend who was miserable in his work, going on about his travails, when I had repeatedly told him he was in the wrong profession to begin with. I finally became very abrupt with him and told him he was a big time loser. That was cutting to the quick, and I meant to—because I wanted to get him to change. In this case, it actually worked. I got him to focus on the solution, not his problems, and now he has a successful and happy life. Sometimes bluntness is necessary to make a point that isn't being heard.

For those of you who have watched *The Apprentice*, you know what goes on in the boardroom. Very often, it sounds like a revved up soap opera with everyone going at each other at once. What you don't see is that sometimes it goes on for hours, and I mean hours. The number of stories, and opinions, and inside dramas that don't make the final cut are truly unbelievable. When it's been edited down enough to fit the hourly format, you see the most important points that were pivotal in allowing me and my advisors to make a decision. The rest of it becomes inconsequential, like background noise—very loud background noise. My point here is that we can all do a little editing our-selves (of our own unnecessary chatter) when it comes to mak-ing a decision.

Stay focused on solutions to problems, not details. That's the power of focus. Use it!

23

DO SOMETHING FOR YOUR COMMUNITY

Trump on the Ocean

People who live in New York City have all heard of Jones Beach. The beach and the boardwalk are part of a fabled history that began with the great Robert Moses—he considered this waterfront park on Long Island as his greatest achievement. I visited Jones Beach as a teenager, and it has always been a special place to me, as it is to thousands of people. So I was delighted when the opportunity came to renovate a major piece of it. When former parks commissioner Bernadette Castro reviewed my plans, she considered them "like a gift from God." We announced this project in September 2006, with a proposed opening in the spring of 2009.

There was opposition at first, from citizens complaining that "Trump was not fit for the Jones Beach scene," and the Society for the Preservation of Long Island Antiquities made it clear they feared what the size of our new building would do to the visual balance of Jones Beach. When they realized how involved I was in the building plans and the fine details, and how concerned I was over the impact of the development on the community and the environment, they were reassured. I even brought out a piece of marble, Breccia Oniciata, to show them. I thought it would look great, and it will. It's the same marble I used at 40 Wall Street; it's sepia and really beautiful.

There will always be naysayers to anything you try to do, but this is a good example of how you can help your community. When they realized how this project would revitalize the local economy, and how beautiful it would be, the negativity lightened up, and most people think it's going to be fantastic. They're right. It will be a win-win situation for everyone. I told people I wanted to bring this historic site up to the gold standard it deserves, to make it a destination point worthy of its amazing history.

What we are doing is replacing the old Boardwalk Restaurant with a beautiful 36,000-square-foot facility that will have Atlantic Ocean and park views. There will be a catering hall and restaurant. We will have social and corporate catering, a restaurant, a lounge, and a ballroom. It will restore Jones Beach to prominence in the life of New York City. In fact, New York can expect to make around $75 million from it over the next 40 years. The building will belong to the state. Not a penny of taxpayer money will be spent.

Our long-term lease required special legislation, which was not a surprise. We're in good company, however—only one other New York parks contract has a term that long—and that's Niagara Falls. We had to deal with a lot of roadblocks, but we prevailed, and it will be a fantastic site.

Being in a position to help out at Jones Beach has been a tremendous feeling. I know detractors will be pleasantly surprised when they see how well integrated the design will be with the environment and the park. In a way, I am paying tribute to Robert Moses—I'm sure he would be very proud—and so will the New Yorkers who have loved Jones Beach.

24

DEFENDING THE FLAG

I have been fighting battles over flying the American flag. Can you believe it? At my California golf club, Trump National Golf Club/Los Angeles, I put up a big American flag and built a flagpole specifically for that purpose. Suddenly they were saying it was too big. Too big? Too big for what? It faces the Pacific Ocean! I think the Pacific Ocean can handle it. I never thought that flying the American flag on American soil would be considered subversive, but that's what it amounted to. Although there will always be some small-minded people who have a complaint to make.

They made their complaints, but then came the backlash. Everyone rallied to my side—in defense of keeping the beautiful American flag waving. The publicity was terrific, not only for patriotism but for my property. Suddenly everyone knew about this beautiful golf course that fronts the Pacific Ocean, and everyone knew that the American flag meant enough to me to go to battle for it. I didn't have to do much persuading to keep the flag—the uproar that ensued did the persuading for me.

So I decided to put up the American flag on my Mar-a-Lago estate in Palm Beach, Florida. I would love to tell the story, but I've agreed with the town not to do so. But I'm pleased to report that the town is happy, I'm happy, and most importantly of all, the flag flies proudly. Always remember—some things are worth fighting for. The American flag is one of them.

25

When Your Wardrobe Malfunctions in Front of 10,000 People, Make It Part of Your Act

Two Public Speaking Screwups

Everyone gets egg on his face sometimes, including me. Screwups may not seem so funny at the time, but at least they make life interesting. Fortunately, in almost every instance, even big goofs can work out for the best. I know that sounds clichéd but it happens to be true.

I was scheduled to speak in Dayton, Ohio, and about 5,000 people were waiting. I was flying in from New York City along with a camera crew, who would be filming the speech for footage on *The Apprentice*. Just as we were ready to take off, my jet stopped. My pilot said there was something wrong with the brakes, and he didn't think it was safe to proceed. So we tried to get a commercial flight—but there weren't any that could accommodate the large group we had. I started to wonder if I might have to cancel the speech. However, when I give my word that I'll be somewhere, I do my best. So what I did was to call all my friends and ask if anyone had a private jet we could borrow. Sure enough, someone had a jet at LaGuardia that wasn't being used. So we all piled out of my jet and into another jet, and finally took off for Dayton. I figured it would all go well from then on.

The Low Point

When we landed in Dayton, it was pouring, just pouring buckets of rain, plus it was rush hour. It was such a mess that they arranged a full police escort for me and my entourage to get from the airport to the arena where I'd be speaking. It still took a long time. This was beginning to seem like a trip to China, not Ohio. To top it off, it was also Melania's birthday, and I had planned to get back to New York City in time to take her out for dinner and to celebrate. Unless she was ready for some midnight supper at a local deli, those plans were about to be scrapped, too. The audience had the worst of it. They had been waiting patiently for several hours at this point.

When I finally arrived, I told the patient folks in Dayton that they'd had their own reality show that day. They were impressed that I had finally made it there despite several major deterrents, and we all had a great time despite the delays, the rain, and the malfunctions. In fact, they sang happy birthday to Melania while they were waiting for me to show up. When I finally arrived, someone gave the heads-up that "Mr. Trump has entered the building"—shades of the days of Elvis. I had a good laugh, and we all had a day to be remembered. The point is, even big goofs can (and often do) work out for the best.

A WARDROBE MALFUNCTION

Another time I was scheduled to speak in Las Vegas in front of approximately 10,000 people, and I flew in from California with about half an hour to spare before going on. Since I had been traveling, I asked a young woman who was the backstage coordinator to have my jacket pressed. So she took my jacket, and I waited in the green room chatting with visitors and with Keith, my bodyguard. When it was time to go on, I started looking for my jacket. It was nowhere to be found. I had 10,000 people waiting for me and no jacket.

The young woman appeared and told us she'd sent my jacket out to a nearby hotel to get pressed, and it wasn't back yet. We were astonished—with a half hour to go before stage time, no one sends a jacket out to be pressed. We thought she'd have it steamed or pressed on the premises, but she was obviously new at this job. I wasn't happy about it, but what could I do? I borrowed Keith's jacket, even though Keith is a bit larger than I am. It had to suffice. I was a few minutes late getting to the stage, but the crowd didn't seem to mind too much. I told them about what had happened backstage, and apologized for a jacket that neither fit nor matched my suit. They didn't seem to mind that either. The speech went well despite the backstage commotion, and they seemed to enjoy the spontaneity that was created by someone's mistake. I still wasn't happy about it, especially since I spend a lot of time preparing to make sure my presentations are seamless, but I figured "what's over, is over," and I let it go.

The next day, on the front page of the major Las Vegas newspaper was a photo and story about me. I shared the front page with a story on Jay Leno. Due to the "wardrobe malfunction" that occurred the night before, they decided to give me more coverage because it ended up being a funny story to them—the billionaire loses his jacket! So, this goof ended up being in my favor in the long run after all.

COACH TRUMP
MAKE IT HAPPEN IN YOUR LIFE

Take blips in stride—instead of trying to deflect problems or obstacles and send them off in another direction, try to embrace them. Turn them into something positive. You can often disarm people this way and get them on your side. Don't get too attached to your ideas. Adjust, adapt, and take things in stride.

26

DON'T GET
COMPLACENT—
THINKING YOU'RE
FOOLPROOF IS A GOOD
WAY TO SET YOURSELF
UP FOR A BIG MISTAKE

How New Trump Projects Happen

The Trump Organization currently has 33 real estate projects in development worldwide. That's a lot of buildings, and managing these projects requires a lot of travel. I'm very grateful that my three eldest children, Don Jr., Ivanka, and Eric are on board now to help out and take trips to places like India,

DJT and Kids

China, Dubai, and Istanbul. My schedule is ballistic enough without those long trips added to it.

Many of these projects are the very desirable Trump International Hotel & Tower combos that incorporate both condominium and hotel accommodations. People often wonder how these buildings get built, and it's a good question since we are the only hotel company that also serves as the developer. If the Trump name is going on a building, there is a huge amount of preliminary due diligence and ongoing management work to be done. The only way to ensure quality is to stay on top of all the issues.

This process is a complex jigsaw puzzle, and there are a lot of factors to consider because we don't allow the Trump name to be associated with anything that hasn't been carefully considered and scrutinized. We receive proposals constantly, all of which are evaluated, but we will not be interested in 99 percent of them. We are also approached by over 300 developers per year who want to partner with us. So we have to take an aggressive approach to evaluating deals. We vet each proposal, analyze the deal, and check out the sites personally. When something is a "go," we review budgets, do predevelopment planning, and then start the bid process. We deal with contractors, subcontractors, and we negotiate the final price. Every construction document has to be reviewed by our team. Next, we start weekly construction meetings and sales and marketing meetings. We speak to representatives on our job sites every single day. Nothing is left to chance. That's one reason for our success.

Because we have many international developments now, one thing we deal with is securing financing in foreign countries. This can sometimes be complicated if the country has a track record of political instability. If we get in at the right point in a real estate growth cycle, it may still be relatively inexpensive to build there, but with good growth potential, so we will take advantage of the opportunity. It would be easy to get complacent because we've had a lot of successes, but we know there is always risk around the corner. We avoid being complacent by being diligent in our preparations. Thinking you're foolproof is a good way to set yourself up for a big mistake.

We very often become interested in a site because I've been there and I see the potential. That happened when I visited Panama City for a Miss Universe Pageant in 2003. I remember saying, "this is a beautiful city, a fantastic place, and I'd like to build something here some day." Well, some day has happened, and the Trump Ocean Club is underway—a 2.4-million-square-foot, 65-story hotel and condominium tower. It's the first time the Trump Organization has invested in Central America, and it's a terrific choice.

As fate would have it, the unveiling of the plans for the Trump Ocean Club, in April of 2006, occurred the same day that Panamanian President Martin Torrijo asked voters to approve a multibillion dollar project to expand the Panama Canal. This would be the canal's biggest modification since 1914, the year it opened, and would enable large, modern cargo ships to navigate the canal. The growth potential was obviously there, and this was a good indication that the city was on the verge of a great surge of interest and activity. The design of the Trump Ocean Club tower is remarkable as well—it appears as a very tall sail, and the units will have flow-through panoramic views—truly spectacular.

I've got my own instincts and preferences but we also review what comes in for us from other people. We cover our bases and are always ready for an opportunity. We are developing a property in Istanbul after my good friend, the late Ahmet Ertegun, the founder of Atlantic Records, suggested the idea. Ivanka will be visiting Turkey to look for a site.

Once a site is approved, we will appoint a project manager to oversee the project. For example, in Las Vegas we have Brian Baudreau to supervise the Trump International Hotel & Towers development. I can call him at any time to see what's happening, and I'll be comprehensively informed from one call. There's an efficiency to our operation that allows us to move forward quickly and confidently.

Trump Ocean Club Panama

No project will be free from the problems that can—and will—surface at any time. However, we do our homework and know we've done our best to ensure a high success rate and a world-famous standard of quality. That's the Trump way, and Don Jr., Ivanka, Eric, and I are working together to make sure it remains that way.

COACH TRUMP
MAKE IT HAPPEN IN YOUR LIFE

Complacency kills. Remember that your success and all good things that come your way are a direct result of your effort; you have a place to live because you've earned it, and you have possessions because you've earned them. Growing cocky or self-assured can lead you directly into a downfall. I know because it's happened to me.

Trump International Hotel and Tower, Las Vegas

27

ONLY IN NEW YORK!

This City Will Serve Up Problems and Solutions You Won't Find Anywhere Else

Traffic can be unbearable in New York City at times. Once I was with *The Apprentice* crew in my limousine, and we got stuck in a traffic jam. We were at a standstill. Everyone started doing their elbow-to-the-horn routine—the horns just kept honking without interruption. My limo was packed, and we hadn't moved an inch in 20 minutes. I finally couldn't stand it anymore. So I decided to get out of the limo and just stand in the middle of the street. What happened was classic, but it worked. Suddenly the horns stopped, there was dead silence because people recognized me standing in the middle of the traffic mess. They did what I hoped they'd do—took their hands and elbows off their horns, and started waving and shouting, "Hey, Donald!" "Hey, it's Donald Trump!" "It's The Donald—Hi, Donald!" It was a great moment, and I waved back and laughed, but mostly I was relieved they'd stopped honking their horns for a couple of minutes at least. There are times when it's great to be recognizable, and this was one of those times. Of course, there are plenty of times when it creates problems I could live without.

I have a great security team, but now and then things can happen. I was scheduled to appear at a party on a ship on the Hudson River that was going to do an evening dinner cruise around Manhattan. It would take up about 15 minutes of my time, and I would leave before the boat left the dock. It was a great cocktail party, and I was talking to a few people, when suddenly I noticed the boat wasn't at the dock anymore—we were going down the river! No one told me we were leaving the dock, including my bodyguard. He hadn't noticed the boat leaving either. Well, here I was, stuck on a cruise around Manhattan for three hours on a Saturday night—not exactly what I had planned! I didn't know who to get angry at first—the captain, my host, my bodyguard, or whoever was around me. I never would have agreed to a three-hour cruise. I thought about jumping in the river and swimming back to Manhattan. I was pretty mad.

Anyway, since there was nothing I could do about it, I decided to go with the flow. It was actually a great group of people, and they seemed happy to have me aboard, whether I'd been invited or not. So I joined them, told some stories, had some laughs, and it was great. It was also a beautiful evening and the party took on a celebratory mood that no one had expected. It ended up being a night we'd all remember.

COACH TRUMP
MAKE IT HAPPEN IN YOUR LIFE

My advice to you is, go with the flow, especially if you don't have a choice. This time I actually enjoyed some smooth sailing that was totally unexpected and not on my agenda. I was thinking, life is like that sometimes. It helped a lot when I just lightened up a bit and managed to have a good time. Try it yourself sometime—you'll find it will work for you whether your name is Donald Trump or not.

28

How to De-Stress

Everyone has his or her own way of letting off steam, letting go of tension, and changing thinking patterns. Whatever works for you is the best choice, as long as it's not self-destructive or destructive to others. That's why I like to golf. Golf is a brain game, but it can be totally relaxing at the same time. I find it opens my mind to new possibilities, and I can problem solve very effectively while I'm on the golf course.

What I do in the office at times is to practice my swing, or I'll just pick up a golf club and think about the game. That action alone is a breath of fresh air—even if it's office air—and helps me see things creatively or in a new light. I know that some people find music or exercise does that for them, but for me it's golf.

Another way to de-stress is to replace negatives with positives. This applies in many areas, for example, I try to surround myself with positive people and get rid of the negative types.

Anyone who visits my office will notice that I have many photographs of my family—my parents, my children, and Melania. That's a great positive focus to keep, not that I need reminders, but a glance now and then can keep things in perspective. I also have photos and mementos of achievements that have meant a lot to me over the years—so if the going is rough, I have tangible reminders of past successes. None of them were easy either.

Keep your momentum going, try to replace negatives with positives, and you'll have more successes waiting for you, even if right now they're nowhere in sight.

29

You Will Be Attacked for Trying to Change Anything

Mar-a-Lago

Marjorie Merriweather Post officially opened her Mar-a-Lago estate in 1927. She was then Mrs. Edward F. Hutton, and she spent four years constructing this incredible estate, which is on a coral reef in Palm Beach, anchored by concrete and steel. For you etymologists, Mar-a-Lago is Latin for sea to lake. Just from those few facts alone, you will begin to get a sense of the history of this magnificent estate, which I saw for the first time in 1985.

We've all heard of love at first sight, and I got that lightning bolt the first time I saw Mar-a-Lago. I immediately knew it had to be mine, all 128 rooms of it, all 110,000 square feet of it, all

Mar-a-Lago

20 acres of it. I knew it might not be easy, but I knew it couldn't
have been easy to build something like this, and the challenges
were apparent. It was a bit of a wreck from neglect, but nevertheless I was determined to own it.

I think you should know a bit about how Mar-a-Lago came
into being, considering it's a historical monument. Ms. Post,
who was the cereal heiress, obviously thought details were
important. Three boatloads of Dorian stone were shipped from
Italy, over 36,000 original Spanish tiles were laid, 2,200 square
feet of black and white marble from an old castle in Cuba were
used for the dining room floor, and a 75-foot tower topped the
main structure. Palm Beach society was under the combined
forces of Mar-a-Lago and Post, and for good reason. This place
surpassed the glory of Newport and San Simeon mansions in a
New York minute. In 1969, the Department of the Interior des-

ignated the estate as a national historic site and the property was placed on the National Register of Historic Places.

After Ms. Post's death in 1973, the estate was transferred, according to her will, to the federal government for use as a presidential retreat or for diplomatic purposes. Ten years later, because there were security concerns as well as a huge maintenance bill, the government conferred the title back to the Post Foundation. Then I came along in 1985.

A lot happened between 1985, which was my first glimpse of this spectacular wreck, until 1995, when it was opened as a private club. Buying the property was the easy part—there weren't too many legitimate offers out there. I paid the Post Foundation a grand total of $8 million for the house and the grounds, including $3 million for all of the original furnishings. This included the china, the crystal, and the goldware. This was a record-setting price, but in reality it was a low price for Mar-a-Lago.

Another reality I was soon to face was the opposition of Dina Merrill, Mrs. Post's daughter. Although she was more concerned with her acting career than the well being of this priceless estate, she did everything she could to thwart me. However, other members of the Post family took my side and realized that I would preserve the integrity and elegance of Mar-a-Lago. One of them, Marjorie Post Dye, the first grandchild and namesake of Marjorie Merriweather Post, referred to me as "a big, blue-eyed guardian angel hovering in a holding pattern just waiting to land and take charge." This family member later told me I had saved Mar-a-Lago. My point is this: You will always have detractors. That's life. The higher you aim, the more opposition you will encounter. In spite of this, there will always be someone who will see your good motives for what they are.

Around Palm Beach, Mar-a-Lago was known as a White Elephant—magnificent, but impossible to maintain. Jimmy Carter gave it back to the Post Foundation because of what it was costing the taxpayers to maintain. As you know by now, I like a challenge. I used the house as a private residence until 1995, but my first thought when I saw it was that it would make a fantastic private club. Along with this great idea came another huge obstacle: zoning and local ordinances would never permit this. It would never happen. It had to remain as a private house, or the property would be subdivided. This was a horrific thought, but that was reality.

I was living very happily with my family at Mar-a-Lago, even though it is far too big as a house. There were parts of it I had never seen. There were bomb shelters, for example, and many wings were left vacant.

THE LOW POINT

Then, in the 1990s I ran into a financial crisis—to the tune of billions of dollars. You can imagine my thoughts—great time to own a money pit! But I can tell you, I didn't actually find it a great weight. I had so much else to worry about that even with its problems Mar-a-Lago felt like a minor weight to me. I remember being in a room full of bankers, trying to work out a very complex situation, and they were friends who were truly trying to be helpful. Trying to be light-hearted in a dire situation, I said to them, "well, since it's Friday, think I'll go down to Mar-a-Lago for the weekend on my 727." They didn't think that was very funny and I knew immediately I'd made a big mistake. So I quickly told them I was going to subdivide Mar-a-Lago, and call it the Mansions at Mar-a-Lago, and promised them it would be a huge moneymaker. That worked! I saw their anger disappear immediately.

However, now I was stuck with doing something about what I'd just promised. The thought of subdividing Mar-a-Lago was anathema to me. I went to Palm Beach with that idea in mind because it was a logical solution to the problem, and I met with the town attorney and the town building inspector. I thought I was entitled to 14 lots, but they suggested I ask for 8, because then the zoning would go through quickly. However, the town rejected my proposal, even though it was a routine proposal, nothing extraordinary or outlandish, and less than what I was entitled to ask for. But I was amiable and went along with whatever they were demanding. I was wondering how long they would continue to try to bamboozle me.

Here's where it's important to stop and think for moment. If you remember, I had hoped to turn Mar-a-Lago into a club in the first place, but I had doubts, big doubts, that it could ever get rezoned as a club. Instead, look what happened: I had been denied my legal right by not being allowed to subdivide the land—I was entitled by law to 14 subdivision lots. I knew this and they knew it, and it was totally unfair. I actually think they were very embarrassed by their hard-nosed stance against me, but it worked to my favor. They might also have known I could take them to court.

You may be right if you're thinking, is anything ever easy for this guy, even if his name is Donald Trump? Doesn't seem so, does it. However, I was determined to set this straight.

As a result of the treatment I got from the city of Palm Beach, my team and I went over everything we had done in the past year and a half and made sure we had complied precisely with every demand. Then we reviewed the actions of the Landmarks Preservation Commission as well as the town council, and we decided to file a $100 million lawsuit. My civil rights had been denied, and we all knew it. I saw a way that this could work to my advantage. That's a good thing to remember when things seem unfair or unjust in your life. That's where keeping cool, being patient, and using your head comes in very handy.

During the litigation, the town council came back to me and said they would give me the 14 lots that I originally wanted—the maximum allowed under the law. So I told them I wasn't interested anymore. What I wanted was a private club. Now I had leverage, due to their mistake. It also turns out that two town council members had the prescience to see what could be done with Mar-a-Lago to make Palm Beach even more desirable, and the town council eventually approved Mar-a-Lago for a private club. This event took longer than a paragraph to describe, but another reason we got approval is that Mar-a-Lago would be open to everyone. There were some clubs in Palm Beach that had no Jewish or African American members. It was hard to believe that, but it was true and I wanted to change that for good. Now we not only had a good case, but a good cause.

Needless to say, this plan brought a whole new group of detractors to the surface. I was prepared for the attack. Every issue became a battle during this time to get Mar-a-Lago going as a club. Once again, however, I knew I was doing the right thing. Once again, I won. In 1995, Mar-a-Lago became a spectacular private club. It has since been referred to as the "Jewel of Palm Beach" and for good reason.

COACH TRUMP
MAKE IT HAPPEN IN YOUR LIFE

You might think I would get tired of all the fighting around Mar-a-Lago. It's a funny thing, but sometimes you find that the more opposition you encounter—or create—by your actions, the more energy you get! Try that approach sometime instead of throwing in the towel or being disgusted when you run into opposition. You'll find out how tough and smart you really are. The actions of the town council, along with the archaic response of the town against a club that admitted all people, gave me a tenacity that could not be beaten. Repeat that to yourself: I'm doing the right thing, and I will not be beaten!

At the same time I was struggling to create Mar-a-Lago, I had many difficulties, obstacles, and setbacks with many other projects as well. I started to learn to expect problems. Experience can give you a resiliency that is very valuable. When you get to that point, remember: Don't give up! Those words can get you to great places, can get you the place you want, and can change attitudes that should be changed. That's winning.

POSTSCRIPT

The latest threat to Palm Beach is from the airport. They want to build a new runway nearby, and it's a real problem. Here's a letter I wrote to the local paper. You have to keep fighting:

March 26, 2007

Mar-a-Lago is a great landmark which would be hurt badly by adding another runway to Palm Beach International Airport. It would destroy the integrity of Mar-a-Lago, and The National Trust for Historic Preservation is in total agreement with that assessment—another runway would be a disaster.

Of equal importance for the city and state government, it is a total waste of $1.5 billion to build a runway that is unnecessary. My pilots and others who are familiar with aviation and the particularities of airports feel it is a complete and total waste of money, as the current runways are adequate, and will be well into the future. They have other land that could be used to build a runway at a different section of the airport if it were really necessary, which it is not.

In short, to build another runway would be destructive as well as wasteful. Save the money and let Bruce Pelly get on with his life.

Donald J. Trump

30

SET THE
RECORD STRAIGHT

Sometimes it pays to take the time to set the record straight. When the *New York Times* published a review of a book that included some juvenile remarks about me, I was inspired to write them a letter. The book review didn't merit a letter, but I enjoy writing when I can set the record straight or make a point. The letter was published by the *New York Times*, and, as it turns out, was named "Best Letter of the Year to the New York Times Book Review" by *New York* magazine.

It may have been a condescending letter but so were the reviewer's remarks. Why did I take the time to write it? Because it mattered and because I don't give up! In fact, here is a copy of the letter for you for future reference—in case this ever happens to you. I hope it doesn't, but remember to do something about it if it does. You just might win a citation for your efforts, in addition to setting things straight. Creating win-win situations for yourself can happen even as a result of bad or negative knocks. That's how you turn problems and challenges into successes.

"BEST LETTER OF THE YEAR TO THE NEW YORK TIMES BOOK REVIEW"

—New York Magazine

August 2005

To the Editor:

I can remember when Tina Brown was in charge of the *New Yorker* magazine and a writer named Mark Singer interviewed me. He was depressed. I was thinking, okay, expect the worst. Not only was Tina Brown dragging the *New Yorker* to a new low, this writer was drowning in his own misery—which could only put me in a skeptical mood regarding the outcome of their combined interest in me. Misery begets misery, and they were a perfect example of this.

Jeff MacGregor, the reviewer of *Character Studies: Encounters with the Curiously Obsessed*—a collection of Mark Singer's *New Yorker* profiles—writes poorly. His painterly turn with nasturtiums sounds like a junior high school yearbook entry. Maybe he and Mark Singer belong together. Some people cast shadows, and other people choose to live in those shadows.

I've read John Updike, I've read Orhan Pamuk, I've read Philip Roth. When Mark Singer enters their league, maybe I'll read one of his books. But it will be a long time—he was not born with great writing ability. Until then, maybe he should concentrate on finding his own "lonely component" and then try to develop himself into a world class writer instead of having to write about remarkable people who are clearly outside of his realm.

I've been a bestselling author for close to twenty years. Whether you like it or not, facts are facts. The highly respected Joe Queenan of the *New York Times Book Review* mentioned in his article of March 20, 2005, "Ghosts in the Machine," that I had produced "a steady stream of classics" with "stylistic seamlessness" and that the "voice" of my books remained noticeably constant to the point of being an "astonishing achievement." This was high praise coming from an accomplished writer. From losers like Jeff MacGregor, whom I have never met, or Mark Singer, I do not do nearly as well. But I'll gladly take Joe Queenan over Singer and MacGregor any day of the week—it's a simple thing called talent!

I have no doubt that Mr. Singer's and Mr. MacGregor's books will do badly—they just don't have what it takes. Maybe someday they'll astonish us by writing something of consequence.

Sincerely,

Donald J. Trump
New York

31

DO GIVE UP—
ON COMPLAINERS

I don't believe the customer is always right. Here's a good example.

I read recently that Sprint-Nextel has cut more than one thousand customers for being too high maintenance. Apparently, these clients call customer service too often and make what the company says are "unreasonable requests."

While the average subscriber calls customer service less than once a month, these 1,200 subscribers getting released by the company call 40 to 50 times more frequently.

All the excessive complaining has frustrated management to the point that the business just isn't worth it anymore. Sprint says they've done what they can to try to resolve the issue but, because the complaints keep coming in, obviously these customers will never be happy.

So they're letting them take their business elsewhere.

I know how they feel. I've had customers I've taken great care of and no matter what I do, they're never happy. So you have to just go about your business and forget about them. Don't keep catering to complainers. A complainer will always be a complainer. They're trouble, plain and simple. They're just not worth it.

32

BE PATIENT—YOU MAY HAVE TO WAIT 20 YEARS FOR A DEAL TO PAY OFF

A West Side Story

What does it feel like to work on something for 20 years? For one thing, it can make you realize that great things don't come easily. Another thing is that it will give you a sense of accomplishment that can't be denied by anyone, even by your most vociferous detractors. I should know, I've had plenty of those. People have often asked me, what keeps you going? In this case, what kept you going on a single development project for three decades?

There's a famous Broadway musical that became an Academy Award winning movie called *West Side Story*. It's considered a classic. The score, the lyrics, and the story are timeless. It also

Trump Place

took 10 years of collaboration between four very gifted people
to get it up and going. I used to think of that when I was trying
to get somewhere with the West Side rail yards in New York,
which have now become Trump Place. Then one day I realized
I'd been working on it for close to 30 years, with no collabora-
tors trying to get this going with me. I was in it alone. I think I
deserve a Tony Award or two for that. But the story itself could
win an award without spinning any yarns—or singing any
tunes—to make it interesting. It's the perfect illustration for
the title of this book: *Never Give Up!*

   This saga began in 1974 when I secured the option to buy
the West Side rail yards from Penn Central Railroad. The city
wasn't doing great, and the West Side wasn't as cool as it is now,
by a long shot, but this was riverfront property and I was getting
it at a very low price. It was my first major deal in Manhattan.

During the next five years, I was busy with my other projects, which included the Commodore/Hyatt renovation, Trump Tower, and Atlantic City. At the same time, government subsidies dropped for the sort of housing I was considering for the location. In addition, I had great opposition from the West Side community, which was notorious for their reluctance to change.

It was a tough situation, and I was busy with other things. So I gave up my original option in 1979, and Penn Central sold the rail yards to someone else. The team they sold it to was smart, but they didn't have much experience in New York. You need a solid knowledge of rezoning, which is a complex fact of the real estate business in this city. They finally got the zoning they needed, but erred in giving too many unnecessary concessions to the city in addition to many other mistakes, and they were forced to sell out. This was a huge development and they weren't prepared for what it entailed, nor did they know how to promote it.

I wasn't surprised to receive a call in 1984 telling me they were interested in selling. I agreed to buy it for $100 million dollars. That's about $1 million per acre for waterfront property in midtown Manhattan. If you consider that the Coliseum site (now the Time Warner Building at Columbus Circle)—which is not too far from the rail yards and is very small in comparison—was sold for $500 million very shortly after I bought the rail yards, you can see that it was a tremendous deal.

That was 1984, and now it's 2007. Trump Place, which is comprised of 16 high-rise residential buildings overlooking the Hudson River is almost finished, but not quite. It has been quite a ride, but let's get back to how it happened.

I realized I'd have to make this project beneficial and attractive to the city in the hope they would give me the zoning I needed. What that would be, I didn't yet know, but by coincidence shortly after I bought the rail yards, NBC announced they were looking to relocate. They'd been at Rockefeller Center for years and were considering a move to New Jersey, which would save them money due to lower taxes and lower real estate prices.

My idea was to offer NBC enough space to comfortably relocate to the West Side while still being able to build my residential project as planned. I then realized the site was ideal for television and motion picture studios, regardless of whether NBC was interested. I decided to call this part of the project Television City. That would attract attention and hopefully generate some excitement. I would also plan to build the world's tallest building on the site and announced that to the press. You can imagine the interest that generated.

Just as had happened before with Wollman Rink, Mayor Koch and his allies were against any and all of my ideas. People said I wasn't being reasonable, but the controversy I stirred up managed to keep this project in the news. I'm big on promotion because promotion works. It helps to get things done. It helps to get the public interested in what will ultimately benefit them. However, the city was stonewalling my project. Koch was still bruised from my success with Wollman Rink, and he certainly didn't want to see me with any more victories.

Let's just say those interim years between 1984 and 1996 were usurped by the ridiculous antics of the city. You've gotten a taste of that already with Wollman Rink. However, this 12-year period is when my tenacity was given a true test. This was the largest development ever approved by the New York City Planning Commission and the biggest project ever undertaken by the private sector in New York City. A couple of times I thought, is this really worth it? Then the challenge itself would keep me going. When I say never give up, that applies to me, big time.

I used seemingly detrimental factors to my benefit: For example, in the early 1990s, things were not good in New York City, but that meant that it was easier to get the zoning I needed. A few years later I started to build in a rising economic climate, which is the ideal situation. Things started looking up. However, it never was easy. Patience is a word not normally associated with me, but you can see that, in fact, it's very much a part of my being. Because I hung in there, we eventually got the approvals we needed and were finally able to break ground in 1996.

Through the years, my plans for this site changed, and Trump Place evolved into a fantastic residential property that has greatly improved the West Side. The 16 high-rise buildings are each unique and very beautiful in their own way, and the community-enhancing 25 acre Riverside Park offers bicycle paths, waterfront walking, picnic and sporting areas, and a pier. It's become a thriving gathering place for the neighborhood, and the buildings sell out before they are finished. It has been a 20-year ordeal, but it's a tremendous feeling to see how it has finally worked out. I think everyone's happy about this one, except maybe for former Mayor Koch. If you visit New York City, be sure to visit the pier and look behind you at the magnificent stretch of buildings along the Hudson River. It's quite a sight.

COACH TRUMP
MAKE IT HAPPEN IN YOUR LIFE

Remember that some things are worth waiting for. Plans can change, sometimes for good reason. Everything has a flip side. Be ready for both sides to surface. Be prepared to wait. Have you waited 20 years for something yet? No? Then complaints will not be accepted. Keep working, keep waiting, and of course—never give up!

33

FRED TRUMP'S FOUR-STEP FORMULA FOR GETTING THINGS DONE

I learned a lot from my father. I learned about competence and efficiency. One of the best pieces of advice he ever gave me was his favorite formula for success. I call it the Four-Step Formula: "Get in, get it done, get it done right, and get out." In looking back, I realize I also learned this by watching him in action. That's how he operated, and it worked.

Some people say that I'm blunt, that I'm brash, that I'm no-nonsense. That's all true. To me, it's a compliment because that's how I get so much done. That doesn't mean that I'm not patient—because I am, but when it's time to get moving on something, the best thing to do is to get moving. I've seen people wait so long for their golden opportunity that by the time they get around to doing something, it's too late.

Let's break this formula down:

1. *Get in* is shorthand for getting started. If you want to be part of the action, you can't watch from the sidelines. Give yourself a goal and focus on it. Write it down. There is a lot of information now that proves that making lists—even if you are able to do it in your mind, which I am—is effective. In fact, three lists should be in your mind at all times: Your daily goals first, your year's goals second, and then your lifetime goals. Look at or think about these lists daily—it will help your focus tremendously. A lot of people don't realize that stress is directly related to loss of focus—so if you learn to control your power of focus, you'll be on the way to conquering stress in your life.

2. *Get it done.* Sometimes that's easier said than done. Here's where you may have to confront obstacles. So, expect them. Expect problems. They are there to bring you closer to getting it done. It's amazing how much this attitude will help you in life—your attitude will be "that's to be expected" versus "poor me, look what's happening!" Keep your focus on getting it done, and your problems will seem like nothing more than part of the day, like sunrise and sunset.

3. *Get it done right.* Here's where I can be—and have been—labeled "difficult." I know what great is. I know what mediocre is. Mediocre and I do not get along. I have high standards for myself, and therefore, I don't put up with less than the best. That's why the Trump brand is synonymous with the best. If you have a product or a brand, or a business, you'd better have the same attitude or

you're not playing hardball. This focus is how I made a name for myself. I have the ability to get things done and to get them done right. Very few people will argue with that fact, whether they like me or not. I can deliver the goods, and they know it. Rock solid is rock solid. Work toward that reputation for yourself.

4. *Get out.* This approach will clear your slate for all the new and exciting projects that are waiting to be done—by you. This is another example of disciplined focus. When a job is finished, it's your time to move on. I have people who will look after my developments, and there is no reason for me to spend my time doing what other people can do. My job is to find new projects for everyone to work on. Figure out what your job is and streamline your activities and mental energy to focus on that.

Considering the scope of my businesses, and the fact that I am actively involved in all of them, I think you can recognize the fact that I employ the Four-Step Formula on a daily basis. Day in, day out, that is how I organize my thoughts and my days. It worked for my father, and it works for me. Make it work for you!

34

THE TURNAROUND ALWAYS STARTS WITH CREATIVE, POSITIVE THINKING

1200 Foreclosed Apartments in Cincinnati

I was thinking about Norman Vincent Peale, so I mentioned him in a speech I gave where my point was that positive thinking really works. Dr. Peale wrote the classic book on this topic called, *The Power of Positive Thinking* (New York: C.R. Gibson, 1956). I attended Dr. Peale's church in New York City, and I heard him speak some years back. What I took away from his speaking is that positive thinking *is* creative thinking. You can't be positive unless you also make an effort to think creatively about your situation. Dr. Peale was a tremendous storyteller, and I also like to tell stories to illustrate a point. This chapter tells the story about how something that's a mess can turn out brilliantly—if you are positive and creative in your approach.

I was always interested in foreclosures and would spend my time in college reading the listings of federally financed housing projects in foreclosure. That's how I found Swifton Village in Cincinnati, Ohio. My father and I bought it together and it became my first big deal. I was still in college.

Swifton Village was in big trouble. There were 800 vacant apartments (out of 1,200), the developers had faltered, and the government had foreclosed. It looked a mess. However, I saw it as an opportunity. Even the fact that there were no other bidders did not discourage me. That's often when you can get the best deals. My father and I put in a minimal bid for Swifton Village. The project had cost $12 million two years earlier, and we paid less than $6 million. We got a mortgage for what we paid, plus close to $100,000, which we'd use to fix up the property a bit. This means we got this project without putting down any of our own money. It would also be possible to cover the mortgage from the rent proceeds.

Our first big challenge was to find tenants who would pay rent. That doesn't sound like an outlandish request, but this complex had a reputation for "rent runners." These tenants would rent a trailer, pile into it with their belongings in the middle of the night, and be gone. They had it down to an art form. I realized we'd have to hire someone for round-the-clock patrol, which we did.

We also wanted to make some improvements because the place was pretty dilapidated. Considering the size of the complex, that would require $800,000. Fortunately, to cover this cost we were allowed to increase the rents immediately, something that was easier in Cincinnati than in New York. Some of the improvements we made included replacing the ugly aluminum front doors on the apartments with colonial white doors. We also put white shutters on all the windows, which considerably improves the aesthetics of a large mass of red brick buildings.

We made sure the grounds were properly landscaped and maintained, and that the apartments were freshly painted and perfectly clean. The change we made was impressive. When we were finished, we ran newspaper ads in Cincinnati. People came and were impressed. In less than a year, Swifton Village was 100 percent rented, and it looked fantastic. It was a beautiful place to live.

The next crucial challenge when you have a complex this size is to find a project manager. We went through at least six or seven before we found a person suited for the job. I'll never forget this man. He wasn't politically correct, he was as incorrect and insulting as they come. He was the personification of a con man. As it turns out, he *was* a con man with a very colorful record of multiple swindles and cons to his credit. But he was a fantastic manager. He could work quickly and get things accomplished. The other managers were perhaps more honest, maybe more affable, but they were ineffective and nowhere near as sharp. I knew I'd have to keep my eye on this guy, but at least things would get done. He also knew how to collect rent, which is not always an enviable job. That's another thing that made him suitable. This wasn't an easy situation from the get go, but it was a great lesson in human nature and looking positively— and creatively—at someone's qualifications. Outwardly the guy looked and acted like a disaster, but he was the one who did the best job.

He got Swifton Village running well enough so that I didn't have to be in Cincinnati very often. I knew he was probably ripping me off, but he kept the place well and people actually paid their rent. The project was a resounding success. A few years later when I was visiting the property, I ran into a tenant who had become a friend. He had survived a concentration camp in Poland so I knew he had street smarts, and I respected his opinion. He told me I should get out, sell the place. It was successful and fully rented, so I ask him why, and he said it wasn't the property or the management, but the area that was turning bad.

I spent a couple days in Cincinnati to check this out for myself, and he was right. It was becoming a rough area, surrounded by equally rough neighborhoods. There was an obvious shift occurring, and not in the right direction. I decided to put Swifton Village up for sale.

Response was swift, and it wasn't long before I saw the fruits of my first big deal. We bought Swifton Village for $6 million and sold it a few years later for $12 million. That's a nice profit. The thing to remember is that I went into this crummy place and decided not only to see it positively but creatively—and look at the results of that attitude. Cultivate it in yourself! Creative, positive thinking can be a powerful source for success.

35

GET THE MOST FROM
EVERY DAY

When I was starting out in Manhattan, I had to be courageous because I was in new territory. I did my homework
and studied and watched what was going on, but I was paving my
own way here and I had to appear confident, or I knew I'd never
make it. Every day mattered, and every day was important. This
was the big time, and I knew it. I've never lost that edge. I still
feel that way every day, and I think that's one reason I've managed to achieve as much as I have.

Confidence can get you where you want to go. It's so much
easier to achieve when you feel good about yourself, your abili-
ties, and your talents. That's why I'm emphasizing confidence as
a way to get the most from every day. It's absolutely essential, so
never let anyone undermine you, including yourself.

Even if you haven't encountered great success yet, there is
no reason you can't bluff a little and act like you have. Confidence is a magnet in the best sense of the word—it will draw

people to you and make your daily life—and theirs—a lot more pleasant.

Take the pains required to become what you want to become, or you might end up becoming something you'd rather not be. It's like the hub versus rim theory—do you want to be the hub, or the rim? Being the hub means you're more centered, more central; being on the rim is being away from the action or the driving force. When I emphasize the importance of focus, that is one way of visualizing it. Focusing on the center, on what's really important in your life, can make the difference between your being the hub or on the rim.

Business is full of complexities. That's what makes it so interesting. Anyone who thinks it's boring hasn't given it much thought. Business can be an art, and as an art, it is evolving and mysterious in its own right. When I wrote *The Art of the Deal*, I was really just illustrating this aspect of business, and I haven't changed my mind about it. Like an artist, I give my utmost every day to what I'm doing. I'm not pretending in any sense of the word.

If you really want to succeed, you'll have to go for it every day like I do. The big time isn't for slackers. Keep up your mental stamina and remain curious. Bored people equal unintelligent people in my mind. Hopefully since you're reading this, that unfortunate group won't ever include you. It better not! I don't like dropouts either. Get with and keep up with the program—and I mean *every day*. I'm not really a tough guy but I am when it comes to education and using your brains. Ignorance is more expensive than education, and considering what's available these days—Trump University, for example—very few people can make a strong case for ignorance.

It was Thoreau who wrote, "If you have built castles in the air, your work need not be lost; that is where they should be. Now put the foundations under them." I couldn't have said it better. Get your vision, get focused, and then do the work—starting today!

36

TAKE A LESSON FROM MUHAMMAD ALI AND ME—KNOW WHEN TO BRAG

Noise versus Substance versus Chemistry

I remember when Muhammad Ali was claiming that he was the greatest. He didn't quibble. He stated in absolute terms that he was the greatest. Fortunately, he proved that he was, or he might have gone down as someone who was delusional. It's interesting to note, now that those days are history, that he set himself up for a situation that demanded that he prove himself, and he did. I think he set the bar high for himself on purpose. I know I do.

I can often be heard saying that my next project is going to be huge and that it will be a tremendous success. Why? First, I have confidence that it will be. Second, I know I have to live up to my own expectations. When you announce something publicly for the world to hear, you'd better be right or the day of reckoning won't be sweet. I don't have to worry about that so much any more, but my standards are such that I give everything the same amount of effort as if it was my first big deal. Plus, announcing a new project always gets my adrenalin flowing.

These public announcements aren't bragging—I simply state the facts. The fact is my buildings are the best. That's why they sell out, very often before they're even built. Trump buildings get higher prices per square foot because they aren't just a brand name, but a luxury brand name. People know what they're getting. The buildings are in demand. Why should I have false modesty when it's false? The same goes for you. If you have something to be proud of and you can back up your claims, then go for it. Let people know. There's no reason to be coy about great accomplishments.

Marketing today requires that we grab the customer's attention. It can make or break a business. I do most of my own public relations because I know how to advertise my own brand. If you have a product or service, learn to do the same. It will save you time and money. If you don't believe in your product and can't talk it up, who will? When people say, "that's not my style," I can understand up to a certain point, but my initial reaction is that maybe they're not too confident about the quality of their work.

I had a young guy come in who had a remarkable background, but he was so self-effacing that I started to believe his attitude more than his accomplishments. I ended up not hiring him because of the dampening effect of his attitude. If he had been a bit more upbeat, I would have been more apt to believe in him. Note what I said—I believed *him*, but I didn't believe *in* him. His attitude overshadowed his qualifications. I don't need to hear someone bragging to be impressed, but someone who is obliterating his own chances seems like a loser to me. I don't want him on my team.

When you go out for interviews, keep that in mind. There's a fine line you have to draw. You may be interviewing with someone who is low key. That's good, keep that in mind. Most people will be able to recognize substance when they see it, but chemistry can't be ruled out either. The young man I mentioned earlier will be a good fit—somewhere else. I have no doubt about it. Remember that sometimes it's just a matter of being on the same wavelength—that old but true fact of personal chemistry. It's an unspoken dynamic that even noise—or substance—can't overrule. It's there or it's not.

37

HOW WOULD I LOOK
WITH A SHAVED HEAD?

Wrestlemania

It became clear to me that wrestling is a very big deal these days, but just as I never thought I'd host *Saturday Night Live*, I never thought I'd get into a ring and take a challenge from Vince McMahon of *Wrestlemania*. But I did. I guess one thing to remember is never *say* never, and never *think* never.

I also never thought I'd agree to have my head shaved if I lost a bet, but I did. Fortunately, I didn't lose, so my famous hair is still there, and it's still famous. Did I have any doubts about winning? I sure did. The challenge was to remain confident and believe I would win. More than 81,000 people turned out to see what would happen.

This was a new arena for me to begin with. Wrestling? I was into baseball when I was in college, and I know a lot about it. I was hardly an expert at wrestling. Which translates to, I had a lot to learn. I like to know what I'm doing, and Vince and I would be picking wrestlers to represent us in the ring.

After much research and consideration, I chose Bobby Lashley, and Vince chose Umaga, both top wrestlers. We had a press conference in Trump Tower a few days before the match, and during the conference, things got a little rough. Vince was taunting me so I belted him, and the next thing we knew Vince was on the floor. My bodyguard jumped out, our wrestlers went on the alert, but we saved the real fighting for the ring. Vince and I had been friends before, but this friendly competition was becoming something else.

The wrestling event set records and was featured in the *New York Times* in a major article. This was big time, and the buzz ran the gamut from die-hard fans who showed up in person to millions watching pay-per-view out of curiosity. What was Donald Trump doing now? Would he really risk getting his head shaved?

I have to admit, there were a few moments when I asked myself the same questions. What was I doing? What was I doing it for? Would the risk be worth it? I stood a very good chance of having my head shaved in public with millions of people watching, some no doubt gleefully. Well, I realized I liked the challenge. I didn't have to get into the ring, but it was still a match. The Battle of the Billionaires is how it was billed, in fact. Vince McMahon is an amazing guy and has been a successful businessman. Because he's an expert in wrestling, I had a few doubts about my ability to choose the right wrestler who would help me see this through triumphantly.

As the buzz increased, I knew there was no turning back. I'd either win or lose. It became that simple. I liked the adrenalin rush that this caused—it was exciting, and I realized I was having a great time. You've got to love what you're doing, as you've heard me say many times before. There was no doubt that I was loving it.

Winning was the icing on top. Not having my head shaved was pretty nice, too. Which shows that it's worth it to take some risks sometimes. This is one of the biggest public chances—and challenges—I've ever taken. Was it worth it? Absolutely. I recommend you take a few yourself. Life's not for the timid. Life's about never giving up. So get into the ring!

38

WHEN YOU'RE
ATTACKED, BITE BACK

A Book and a Lawsuit

When you've spent 40 years building a brand that is known worldwide, and then someone publishes a book that denounces your worth and damages your image and reputation, and in a scathing way, it becomes a serious issue.

There is a writer with the *New York Times* named Tim O'Brien who had written some very negative articles about me. I didn't like him, and I didn't respect him as a writer because his facts were so incorrect and his articles were so viciously negative. Then I heard he was doing a book about me—and I was told he would write it with or without my cooperation—so it seemed in my best interests to work with him so his facts would be correct. I already knew he was bad news, but I was very cordial and open with him, giving him interviews, and having him travel with me on my jet so I could give him the time he needed. I extended every courtesy to him, especially that of time.

Then his book, *Trump Nation*, came out, and I realized there's a difference between bad news and evil. This guy was despicable. His intent was defamation. I'm not sure what he was writing about, because what he wrote is so far from the truth, but I do know what he was writing for: attention and money. This isn't the proper way to do that.

He had outright lies in his book, and he intended to damage me personally and my businesses. His reporting was reprehensible, and as a writer he is not very talented. I decided not to look the other way and toss it off as jealousy, malice, or greed. Instead, I sued him and the publisher for a lot of money. The writer got the attention he was obviously looking for, but his publisher got something they weren't looking for. They obviously didn't know they were dealing with a guy who would eventually write *Never Give Up*—and actually mean it. The publisher's conduct was not much better than O'Brien's, and they will have to bear the consequences.

There are all types in the world. I've known some terrific writers and journalists who are honest and dedicated to their profession. Even though this guy wrote badly about me in the past as a *New York Times* reporter, I like to give people the benefit of the doubt, or at least a chance. In this case, I was giving him a second chance, in fact *more* than a second chance, considering the negative articles he'd already written about me. So take this as a warning—they are going to pay a big price.

For example, this writer purposely and knowingly understated my net worth by billions of dollars. He insisted I was worth a couple hundred million dollars, at most. Even *Forbes* acknowledges I'm worth much more, $2.7 billion being their conservative valuation. This writer had access to all the facts, but chose to ignore them. Instead of relying on those facts, he claimed he was relying on anonymous sources to misrepresent my business. So what I did was to invite *Forbes* in to investigate, to go over everything, which they did meticulously, and they confirmed what they had originally found—that I was worth, conservatively, $2.7 billion. They published their findings. All this time and effort put out by the *Forbes'* team and my team was a direct result of *Trump Nation*'s deliberate reporting errors designed to damage my reputation and businesses. As of September 2007, *Forbes* confirmed my worth at $3 billion. That number is much less than my actual net worth but they were being very conservative.

By way of comparison, a very respected journalist and writer, Robert Slater, wrote a book about me—*No Such Thing as Over-Exposure*—that turned out wonderfully for everyone. I had extended to Bob actually less hospitality than I had to Tim O'Brien, but because Bob is a writer of integrity, the end result was terrific. Bob has great credentials, having reported for both *Time* and *Newsweek* for many years, and he is one of the world's leading business biographers. He also seems to understand that getting the facts right is part of a journalist's job.

In any event, I told the publisher I had no interest in settling without a large payment and a full apology. I do not mind paying large legal fees as long as the end result will be the truth, which is something they are avoiding. Many people would say, why bother? I say, why give up? I do not back down. I don't need the money from winning the case—I need to set the record straight and maybe make it harder for other disreputable writers to knock people for the fun or profit of it. I told them it was a court case that I am truly looking forward to, because that's the truth.

39

PRIME REAL ESTATE FALLS INTO THE PACIFIC—NOW WHAT?

Trump National Golf Course in Palos Verdes, California

I've always said I liked challenges, and when I decided to take over the beleaguered Ocean Trails Golf Course in Palos Verdes near Los Angeles, that's exactly what I got. I began referring to it as Ocean Trials before renaming it Trump National Golf Club, and for good reason. In an article in *Fairways and Greens*, they described the 18th hole, which, by the way, is the one that slid into the ocean, as Ground Zero plus $61 million. Can you believe I spent $61 million on one hole? Well, believe it. When I want something done, I want it done right.

This hole is the most expensive in golf history. I would hope so because I can't imagine doing this too many times. If you saw

Trump National Golf Club

the situation through my eyes, you would see that it warranted every penny I spent. The course fronts the Pacific Ocean for two miles and easily rivals the fabled Pebble Beach in both beauty and finesse. I could see that before it became a reality, and so I didn't care about the expense involved. Golf courses are works of art and deserve that kind of attention.

As with many of my projects, I'd been paying attention to this course for years. I knew it had the potential to be one of the top tier golf courses of the world. However, when it opened as Ocean Trails in 1999, there was a catastrophe when the 18th hole slid toward the ocean, also damaging three adjacent holes. The water lines, which were beneath the fairway, had given away. This was a very serious mess. A landslide is a nightmare for a cliffhanging property. Especially when it involves 17 acres of earth. Suddenly, an 18-hole course was reduced to a 15-hole course.

It was a disaster for the owners, and they entered bankruptcy court in 2002. That's when I made my move and offered them $27 million for the land, the clubhouse, and the course.

Compare that to $61 million for one hole. It was a good deal. I had to make a choice—should I just fix it and be done with it because it was already a nice enough course—or should I go all out and make it over into one of the most celebrated courses in the world?

I think you can guess which choice I made. It wasn't the easy choice, but it was the best one. I estimated that to redo the entire course, including reconstruction of the fallen hole, would cost me around $265 million. So how do I explain $61 million for one hole? Well, this was what was involved: A series of walls, made from local Palos Verdes rock quarried at $600 a ton, and a structural layer built underneath the hole that goes down the cliff to the beach, which means that every 10 feet is a steel platform—which provides a very strong structure. This was intricate and difficult work.

I will admit I had some second thoughts about spending that much on one hole. That's a huge investment, no matter how much money you have. And the difficulties were astounding. What I did was something that I would suggest to you: Look at the solution—not the problem. I focused on the spectacular outcome I wanted, and it got done. I had moments of doubt, when I wondered how feasible my "think big" attitude was going to be in this situation, and where it might lead me. Well, I guess I like cliffhangers because it definitely had that feeling about it.

On the positive side of things, I brought in Pete Dye, one of the legends in golf course design, to remake Ocean Trails into a worthy rival to Pebble Beach. If anyone in the industry could do that, Pete Dye could. I wanted to make this course the best, and we completely redesigned it. It's brand new. It includes waterfalls and a great driving range. In order to build the driving range, I had to wipe out about 30 housing lots to have the appropriate space. That means about $300 million because each lot would bring about $10 million—so all these things had to be considered. Also, everything was new, from the traps and sand to the tees and fairways. I wanted crushed granite for the bunkers. The costs were enormous, and I was hoping the rewards would be too. I was enjoying myself, but would this work and expense pay off? Would this be just a great experiment—great expectations that don't manage to deliver?

I have to stop here to say that there are no guarantees in anything. People see my successes and really think it's a breeze to get it all done. It's not, and I spend plenty of time assessing, reassessing, analyzing, and scrutinizing. People just don't see me doing that. Another important thing to consider is experience— I've been a developer for a long time, so a lot of decisions are second nature to me and not a terrific demand on my brainpower to figure out. I can move quickly once I've done the groundwork in my mind. However, the plans have to be in place. Be sure you have a foundation of expertise and experience in whatever you do, and then you can act decisively and creatively.

There were a lot of details to consider along with the reconstruction of the golf course itself. The 40,000-square-foot clubhouse, for one thing, which has a restaurant that has won the Golden Scepter Award (Best New Restaurant) and the Golden Bacchus Award (for its wine list). The course itself has become the number one golf course in California, and the Michael Douglas & Friends Pro-Celebrity takes place there every April. Trump National Golf Club Los Angeles has become a spectacular success on all levels. You might even call it a landslide. But my *never give up* moment came when, after knowing the potential of the property for years, I saw that landslide disaster and wanted to do something spectacular about it. Thinking big? What a great idea. . . .

40

THINK
INTERNATIONALLY

Y ou've heard me emphasize the importance of keeping
informed about global events, which includes political as
well as financial news. I'd like to recommend to you a book that
was published in 2007 that reinforces the importance of thinking internationally. It's called *Microtrends: The Small Forces
Behind Tomorrow's Big Changes*. It's written by Mark J. Penn who
is a highly respected analyst who has been an adviser to Fortune
500 corporations and to many foreign heads of state. He has an
insight into both national and international trends and events
that shape our future. Bill Gates said, "Penn has a keen mind
and a fascinating sense of what makes America and the world
tick, and you see it on every page."

Penn has a chapter on international home buyers. Being in
real estate, I took a special interest in what he had to say. Penn
astutely points out that foreign ownership of residential real

TRUMP: NEVER GIVE UP

estate in the United States is a hot trend. Globalization has torn down the barriers that have formerly separated the national from the international markets and one result is that affluent foreigners have been drawn to real estate in the United States. I recognized this years ago, which he points out:

> In New York, Donald Trump was a major factor in opening up the city to foreigners. Most buildings in New York City had been co-ops, and since co-ops can reject anyone for just about any reason, they looked very carefully at absentee foreign purchasers. But Trump opened condos, and sales of condos are largely unregulated because they offer single apartments, not share in a corporation. Now that most new buildings are condos, foreign buyers are streaming in.

The important thing to consider is that more and more there is an interdependence of world economies. No one can afford to be isolationist anymore. For many years, many Americans have had second homes in foreign countries, and now the trend, as Penn points out, has hit our shores. This is nothing new, but it's relatively new to us. I think it's a harbinger of things to come, and when I first went with condos years ago, I knew it was a timely thing to do.

My point is, I had been keeping up with global events for years, and it wasn't that hard for me to see this trend coming. I'm not clairvoyant, but I take the time to be well informed. You can and should do the same thing. Spend some time on international events, read books, and keep ahead of what's happening. Catching up can waste a lot of time—having some prescience can save you a lot of time. Keep your focus global and you may very well find yourself ahead of the game.

41

WHERE OTHERS FAIL—THERE'S YOUR OPPORTUNITY

A Wall Street Story

On occasion, I am asked what my favorite deals have been. I have a lot to choose from, but there is something about the acquisition of 40 Wall Street that will always stand apart. Not only because of the location, which is in the financial district of Manhattan, but because of an almost magical sense of timing, which made it seem like destiny. That does not mean it was an easy, simple feat to acquire it, because it wasn't, but I like to use this as an example to tell people about how difficulties and challenges can add another dimension to your life—and a positive dimension at that.

In addition to being the tallest building in lower Manhattan, 40 Wall Street is a 1.3-million-square-foot landmark. I got it for

40 Wall Street

$1 million. Even people who know very little about real estate can be duly impressed with that price. I'll tell you some background about how it came about because it's a great story. It will also illustrate the myth of so-called overnight successes. I had been watching this building for decades, and I knew a lot about it before making my move.

In the 1960s and 1970s, 40 Wall Street was a fully occupied building, and it was indeed a hot property. However, in the early 1980s, it was bought by Ferdinand Marcos, the former dictator of the Philippines. Unfortunately, a revolution in the Philippines required his full attention, and the skyscraper at 40 Wall Street fell into decline. Dealings became chaotic, and soon the whole thing was a mess. Marcos was out.

Then the Resnicks, a great real estate family, descended on 40 Wall Street, but after a long period of negotiation, it became clear that the Resnicks and their partner Citibank weren't going to make it, and 40 Wall Street would once again be back on the block. They were unfortunate to be dealing with one of the dumbest bankers I have ever known, Patricia Goldstein. But for me this was good news. I wanted very much at this time to make my move, but this was the early 1990s and I was in no position to do so. The market was terrible, and in addition, my own financial woes were exactly that—woeful. I remember thinking that I'd love to acquire this building, but I thought it was one of those dreams that would never come true. This is a good lesson for those of you who have thought that way too. Shortly after I had just about given up on my dream, something happened.

It was announced that the Kinson Company, a group from Hong Kong, was buying 40 Wall Street. They made a great deal. After their purchase was complete, I called them and said I'd like to meet them about a possible partnership. As it turns out, they weren't interested in a partnership but in making 40 Wall Street the downtown equivalent of Trump Tower—with an atrium. What they would do with the steel columns that held up the 72-story building never seemed to enter their minds. I was truly astounded. But it also gave me some hope—they obviously didn't know what they were doing. How long could they continue to hold on to a building that dwarfed them in every conceivable way?

The Kinson Group did prove to be relatively clueless about renovating, running, and leasing out a New York City skyscraper. To begin with, they weren't in the real estate business, they were in the apparel business. Kinson began pouring tens of millions of dollars into the building and getting absolutely nowhere. They had problems with tenants, contractors, suppliers, architects, even the owners of the land under the building, the Hinneberg family. Eventually, they wanted out, and they called me. I was thrilled.

Three years of dealing with a situation out of their depth had taken a toll on Kinson. It was now 1995, and the market still wasn't so good. Kinson had every reason to want to get out, and they wanted to do so quickly and quietly. I was in a great position due to their distress, and the negotiations began, with me offering them $1 million in addition to assuming and negotiating their liens. I also made the deal subject to a restructured ground lease with the Hinneberg family.

They accepted my terms without question—they obviously just wanted out and fast. Sad as their story is, it's true to New York real estate—if you don't know what you're doing, you simply won't make it. That's another good lesson to remember: always know what you're getting into—you have to do your due diligence, especially if it's a field that's new to you.

The next thing I did was to call Walter Hinneberg himself in Germany, then I flew over to meet him. I got along very well with the Hinnebergs, and they realized that after a string of losers who had owned the building, I had the integrity of their spectacular property first and foremost in my mind. They are a truly great family, and they knew I loved the building, that I would be doing everything possible to restore it to its inherent grandeur. We worked out a new lease for the land under the building, extending the term to over 200 years, and the agreement was modernized, which served everyone's best interest. However, keep this in mind—getting to this point was a long time coming. It didn't happen overnight. I was tenacious and attentive to this property for many years.

Then the question was what to do with the building. I had been advised to turn it into a residential property by almost every person who had an educated opinion to give. However, I felt in my gut that I wanted to keep it as a great business address, because Wall Street *is* a great business address, so I refused to budge. Time has shown that I made the right decision—it is a thriving and sought-after building, with many of the top-notch businesses in the world operating within its walls.

In addition, very soon after acquiring 40 Wall Street, the real estate market turned for the better, and the downtown area experienced a renaissance in both commercial and residential properties and developments. The timing could not possibly have been better. I'm not one for miracles, but this comes close.

I make approximately $20 million a year in rentals from 40 Wall Street and the building is now worth $500 million. Not bad for a $1 million investment. So, aside from owning the most beautiful building in lower Manhattan, I have the added attraction of making a profit. Have you been to the Trump Building at 40 Wall Street? If you have, you know why I'm so proud. There is nothing like Wall Street, and there is nothing as beautiful as this building.

COACH TRUMP
MAKE IT HAPPEN IN YOUR LIFE

Nothing is easy. Sometimes you just have to be stubborn as well as patient.

Recognize opportunity—it always hides behind problems and ugliness and failure—especially the failures of others. Every challenge or obstacle you come up against is simply an opportunity in disguise. Think big, think creatively, and you'll see it.

And don't forget your gut instinct—it's there for a reason.

APPENDIX A

Trump's Top 10 List for Success

If you've heard me speak, you may have noticed I emphasize several things repeatedly—never give up is one, being passionate is another, keeping focused is up there, and keeping your momentum runs a close fourth. I've learned those things from experience.

Here's the complete top 10 list I give when I speak at colleges:

1. *Never give up!* Do not settle for remaining in your comfort zone. Remaining complacent is a good way to get nowhere.

2. *Be passionate!* If you love what you're doing, it will never seem like work.

3. *Be focused!* Ask yourself: What should I be thinking about right now? Shut out interference. In this age of multitasking, this is a valuable technique to acquire.

4. *Keep your momentum!* Listen, apply and move forward. Do not procrastinate.

5. *See yourself as victorious!* That will focus you in the right direction.

6. *Be tenacious!* Being stubborn can work wonders.

7. *Be lucky!* The old saying, "The harder I work, the luckier I get" is absolutely right on.

8. *Believe in yourself!* If you don't, no one else will either. Think of yourself as a one-man army.

9. *Ask yourself: What am I pretending not to see?* There may be some great opportunities right around you, even if things aren't looking so great. Great adversity can turn into great victory.

10. *Look at the solution, not the problem.* And never give up! Never never never give up. This thought deserves to be said (and remembered and applied) many times. It's that important. Good luck!

APPENDIX B

Trump's Rules for Negotiating

Negotiating is an art. There are nuances and finely honed techniques and rules to be aware of. Here are a few of them:

- *Know what you're doing.* Sounds simple, but I've seen a lot of instances where I couldn't believe how much the other side didn't know. I immediately knew I could have a grand slam and fast, just based on their apparent lack of preparation. My father used to tell me, "Know everything you can about what you're doing." He was absolutely right, and I'm giving you the same advice. Follow it.

- *Remember, it takes a lot of smarts to play dumb.* This is a good way to see how much your negotiating partners don't know. It's also a good way to see if they are bulldozing you.

- *Keep them a bit off balance.* What they don't know won't hurt you, and that may help you down the line. Knowledge is power, so keep as much of it to yourself as possible.

- *Trust your instincts.* There are a lot of situations that will not be black and white in negotiating, so go with your gut. Combine this with your homework and you'll be ahead of the game.

- *Don't be confined by expectations.* There are no exact rules, and sometimes I've changed course in the middle of negotiations when something new has occurred to me. Remain flexible and open to new ideas, even when you think you know exactly what you want. This attitude has provided me with opportunities that I would not have thought about before.

- *Know when to say no.* This has become instinct for me by now, but I think we all know when that buzzer goes off inside. Pay attention to that signal.

- *Be patient.* I've waited for some deals for decades, and it was worth the wait. But make sure what you're waiting for is worth it to begin with.

- *To speed up negotiations, be indifferent.* That way you'll find out if the other side is eager to proceed.

- *Remember that in the best negotiations, everyone wins.* This is the ideal situation to strive for. You will also be laying the groundwork for future business deals with people who know what integrity is.

In summing up, I can say that negotiation is an art. All the arts require discipline, technique, and a dose of imagination to take them beyond the realm of the ordinary. Don't be an ordinary negotiator when you can be an extraordinary one. Devote time to this art and it can bring you enormous rewards.

INDEX

Stage fright, 55
Standards, high, 136–137
Starting over, 91–94
State Theater at Lincoln
    Center, 51
Stress relief, 115–116
Success:
  lack of, 36
  preparing for, 34–35
  top 10 list for, 165–166
Survivor, 8–9
Swifton Village, 139–141

T

Technology, as global business
    driver, 76–77
Television City, 133
Thinking:
  internationally,
      157–158
  positively, 3–4, 115,
      138–141
Thoreau, Henry David, 143
Tiffany and Company, 30, 31
Time Warner Building, 132
Torrijo, Martin, 109
Tortoises, gopher, 60
Traffic problems,
    112–113
Trump, Don, Jr., 22,
    106–107, 110

Trump, Donald J.:
  advice, best piece of, 38
  charity activities, 24–27,
      38
  childhood ambitions, 36
  dessert, favorite, 35
  discovery, sense of, 69–70
  fear of failure, 37, 83–88
  financial turnaround, 1–4,
      6
  frequently asked questions,
      34–38
  happiness, sources of, 38
  inspiration for ideas, 36
  instincts, 9–11
  lunch habits, 35
  movie, favorite, 38
  negotiating rules, 167–168
  New York Times, letter to,
      125–127
  real estate goal, 37–38
  rising time, 38
  school subject, favorite, 38
  success, top 10 list for,
      165–166
  vacations, 37
  VISA commercial, 90
Trump, Eric, 25, 106–107,
    110
Trump, Fred C.:
  on Commodore Hotel, 63
  Four-Step-Formula,
      135–137